THE ART OF
THE MOVING PICTURE

THE ART OF THE MOVING PICTURE

INTENDED, FIRST OF ALL, FOR THE NEW ART MUSEUMS
SPRINGING UP ALL OVER THE COUNTRY. BUT THE
BOOK IS FOR OUR UNIVERSITIES AND INSTITUTIONS
OF LEARNING.   IT CONTAINS AN APPEAL TO OUR
WHOLE CRITICAL AND LITERARY WORLD, AND TO OUR
CREATORS OF SCULPTURE, ARCHITECTURE, PAINTING,
AND THE AMERICAN CITIES THEY ARE BUILDING.
BEING THE 1922 REVISION OF THE BOOK FIRST
ISSUED IN 1915, AND BEGINNING WITH AN AMPLE
DISCOURSE ON THE GREAT NEW PROSPECTS OF 1922

By V A C H E L   L I N D S A Y

Introduction by

STANLEY KAUFFMANN

" Hail, all ye gods in the house of the soul, who weigh Heaven and
Earth in a balance, and who give celestial food."

*From the book of the scribe Ani, translated from the original
Egyptian hieroglyphics by Professor E. A. Wallis Budge.*

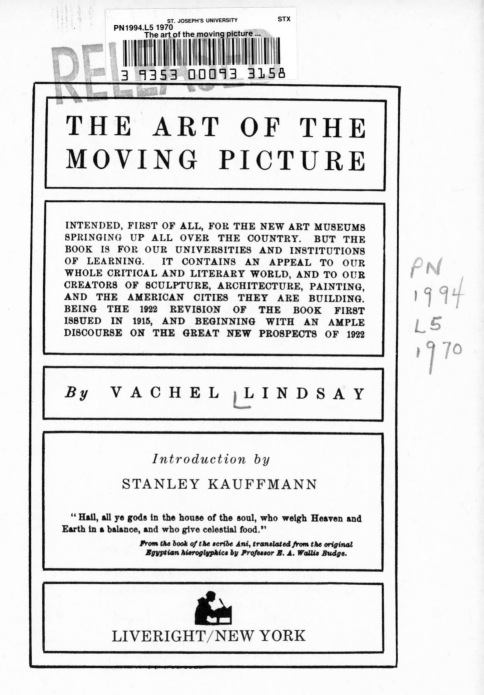

LIVERIGHT/NEW YORK

SBN 87140-508-3 CLOTHBOUND
SBN 87140-004-9 PAPERBOUND
LIBRARY OF CONGRESS CATALOG CARD NUMBER 75-114381

MANUFACTURED IN THE UNITED STATES OF AMERICA

CONTENTS

CONTENTS

INTRODUCTION
by Stanley Kauffmann

"This is a joyous and wonderful performance," said Francis Hackett when he reviewed this book in the *New Republic* of December 25, 1915. He then went on to call it "a bold and brilliant theory, really bold and really brilliant, and takes first place as an interpretation of the greatest popular aesthetic phenomenon in the world."

Hackett was certainly not alone in praising the book. Gordon Craig, the great man of the theater whom Lindsay urges to enter films, wrote to the author from Rome suggesting that they found a film studio together. D. W. Griffith was moved to ask Lindsay to be his guest at the New York premiere of *Intolerance*. Victor O. Freeburg, who taught what surely must have been one of the first college film courses—at the School of Journalism of Columbia University—used the book as a text. Herbert Croly, the editor of the *New Republic*, invited Lindsay to be the magazine's film critic. (Lindsay wrote occasional reviews during 1917.) Comment on the book was wide and intense.

But it has virtually disappeared. Although most film historians know the book, very few contemporary film enthusiasts, in my experience, are even aware of its existence. It has been out of print for many years. The revised edition of 1922, reprinted here, is scarcer than the original of 1915. Lindsay's biographers pay it scant attention. Edgar Lee Masters, who published a biography of Lindsay in 1935, disparages *The Art of the Moving Picture*. Eleanor Ruggles, who published a biography in 1959, does not deal with it in any significant way. Yet, out of the mass of Lindsay's poetry and prose, this may be the work most worthy of survival. And in the field of film aesthetics, it is the first important American work, still important.

In several ways it is dated and cranky. It is hyperbolic and self-appointedly supreme. (Just glance at the table of contents, under Book II.) But its hyperbole and its large claims are not matters really of blindness or conceit, they are right out of the best in Lindsay's character, which dealt mainly in largenesses, and out of his enthusiasm for the film, which insisted and insisted, and was right.

Nicholas Vachel Lindsay was born in his family's house in Springfield, Illinois, in 1879 and died in the same house in 1931. For this man to whom the everyday was magical, Springfield itself was "the mystic, where I always live, wherever I may be." His father was a physician; his mother was active in religious missionary work. His parents sent him to a sectarian college in 1897, but he left in 1899, having found what he thought was, for him, a better vocation to express Christ. He wrote to his parents: "Now that I have found it must be Art, I must learn to preach my purpose into other artists."

He spent four years studying painting at the Art Institute in Chicago, then moved on to New York where he studied for another year under Robert Henri. (Among his fellow-students were Rockwell Kent, George Luks, and George Bellows.) He had long been interested in poetry, had begun to write it, and now began to show it to magazines. Then, on Henri's kindly but firm advice, he turned away from painting and concentrated on poetry. He had no luck in trying to place an illustrated book of his poems with a publisher, so he took a dramatic step. In March, 1905, he printed one hundred copies each of two of his poems at his own expense. "Inspired," says Miss Ruggles, "by the stories of President [Theodore] Roosevelt—who, when up against stubborn opposition, was said to bypass the entrenched powers and go with his case straight to the people—and also by the troubadors of old," he put the poems in his overcoat pocket and went out into the streets of New York to sell them. Possibly, too, he had been influenced by his mother's missionary example.

Lindsay was a fool, of course, as some of this book is foolish; but it was foolishness on a scale and out of a fire that triumphs over common common-sense. The poet says in Shaw's *Candida*, "Do you think that the things people make fools of themselves about are any less real and true than the things they behave sensibly about?" His reception in the New York streets and shops was varied, to put it mildly, but the idea of direct bardic communication never died in him. Subsequently he made three great journeys through America on foot, carrying and reading his poems on the principle in the title of one of his collections: *Rhymes to be Traded for Bread*. In the spring of 1906 he walked from Florida to Kentucky; in April and May of 1908 he walked from New York to Ohio; and in the summer of 1912 he walked from Illinois to New Mexico. In later life he kept up his direct contacts on recital platforms around the United States and also abroad; in those early days he was knocking at farmhouse doors

to sell his poems, and working in the fields for
food when interest in the muse was low.

At the age of 30, he was back in Springfield,
unsuccessful and unsettled; and the neighbors
pitied poor Dr. Lindsay, the father of such an
aimless son. But in the summer of 1910 the poet
wrote, illustrated and spent his last cent to publish *The Village Magazine*—only one issue—and
circulated the 700 copies to good effect. Elsewhere
he began to publish such poems as "The Eagle
That Is Forgotten", "General William Booth Enters into Heaven" and "The Congo", and he began
to be known. His first book was published. He
gave poetry readings, east and west, and was
highly successful on the platform. John Dos Pas-
sos, who heard him at Harvard in 1915, said, "We
went to kid, but were very much impressed in
spite of ourselves." Then, suddenly, out of this
dynamic, handsome, dramatic poet came a book
on film aesthetics.

Helped by hindsight, we can see why. First, his
love of films is evidenced by his poems to movie
stars. (In addition to the three he mentions, there
is an "Epitaph" for the comedian, John Bunny).
Second, he had a highly cultivated visual sensi-
bility; he felt that an interest in that kind of sensi-
bility was being slighted in America, and that the

THE ART OF THE MOVING PICTURE

film could be a wonderful restorative. And third, which must have figured in his consciousness, the film could do with titanic ease what he had been trying to do literally on his own two feet: spread the gospel of Beauty (still, in those days, to be spelled with a capital B), educe some national standards, and thus perhaps create a whole out of a huge and heterogeneous nation.

The Art of the Moving Picture is astonishing, as a work of analysis and vision. Over fifty years ago Lindsay saw the hunger that still obsesses the film enthusiast:

> I'm delighted to affirm that not only the *New Republic* constituency but the world of the college and the university where I moved at the time, while at a loss for policy, were not only willing but eager to take the films with seriousness.

As the present incumbent of the *New Republic* post, I can affirm all parts of the statement today, not least the desire for policy. All the eminent writers on film aesthetics from Lindsay and Bela Balazs to the present have contrasted the appetite for film with the absence of any reliable body of aesthetics—any canon from which one can at least depart. In my view, no film aesthetician has filled the gap nor—for reasons too complex to discuss here—is likely to fill it: I foresee no Aristotle of film; but Lindsay at least took the first strong step toward analysis.

Obviously, there is no merit in categories, as such. Lindsay was interested in opening up powers, in showing possibilities to film-makers, in showing possible demands and rewards to film-goers.

His three fundamental categories—which he calls "foundation colors"—are Pictures of Action, of Intimacy, and of Splendor. They are still the foundation colors of film, sometimes subdivided and often blended, but still fundamental. He saw Action in the basic cinema manifestation of the chase, but he saw further that the Action film is a species of abstraction: as, for instance, "the gesture of the conventional policeman in contrast with the mannerism of the stereotyped preacher." The Intimate Picture, which today is probably our dominant mode, is not merely or not at all a work of greater realism, it proceeds *through* realism and naturalism toward an interiorism of "elusive personal gestures". The Splendor film he saw as "the total gesture of crowds", the film in which peoples, races, and history are the elements of drama.

Sculpture-in-motion, painting-in-motion, architecture-in-motion, are what he also calls these three types; but these are very much more than facile phrases. They are nuggets out of which he refines subtle perceptions. He also applies the traditional poetic categories to these film types: dramatic, lyric, epic. His point is to show continuity and advance: to show that the film is bound, conceptually and formally, to the past, but that it takes those concepts and forms into new dimensions. He is also quite patently propagandizing—giving (rightful) dignified affinities to an art that was being superciliously patronized by many of those who flocked to it.

The development of the book often tempts us to think of Lindsay as naive. All that talk of Fairy Splendor and Patriotic Splendor! More frequently, however, he pierces to the root or to the future. He understood the aesthetic fallacy that his friend Freeburg hammered in the first sentence of his own book: "It is a common error to judge the photoplay by the standards of the stage drama and to condemn it because it cannot do exactly what the stage drama can do." Lindsay not only saw the special powers of the stage but the special provinces of film. *The Cabinet of Dr. Caligari* (the importance of which he recognized at once) "proves in a hundred new ways the resources of the film in making all the inanimate things which, on the spoken stage, cannot act at all the leading actors in the film."

His fascination with hieroglyphics, in connection with film, antedates Eisenstein's cognate fascination with the Japanese ideogram (in *Film Form*). Lindsay sees, in 1915, the revolution in human perception involved in the very existence of film. There is a clear prediction of McLuhan in: "Edison is the new Gutenberg. He has invented the new printing." Lindsay sees, in 1915, the quintessence of the *auteur* theory of film criticism, formulated some forty years later: "An artistic photoplay . . . is not a factory-made staple article, but the product of the creative force of one soul, the flowering of a spirit that has the habit of perpetually renewing itself."

He foresees film schools, film libraries and archives, documentaries, the use of film for instructional purposes. He foresees the need for an American tradition of serious film. He even foresees the sales film and TV commercial: "Some staple products will be made attractive by having film-actors show their uses."

He is certainly not free of false judgment and false prophecy. His animus against the musical accompaniment of silent films (he thought people should converse while watching pictures) is sheer quirk—and he is generous enough to quote a story against himself. His ideas on the sound-film—which, in crude form, is as old as the silent—are as unimaginative as most of the book is visionary. (His prejudices against sound and dialogue reflect his painterly education—a prejudice towards the eye alone that antedates some of the shortcomings of the modern "visual" school of film criticism.) His drama analysis—dividing the theater into ancient, English, and Ibsenite traditions —is less simplifying than simplistic. His chapter on the screen as a possible substitute for the saloon can only be seen—with utmost charity—as the view of a man who worships Dionysus in his own way. And this catalogue of oddities is not complete.

But with all the oddities, the bad guesses, the exaggerations of prose and of judgment, the embarrassing touches of a much lesser Whitman, this book is a considerable marvel. Lindsay had a clear sense that a profound change was taking place, not only in cultural history but in all human histories—the external and also the most secret. He felt lucky to be alive at that moment. And, poet and evangelist that he was, he saw some fundamental ways to understand and *use* the change. Francis Hackett concluded his review in 1915: "He has initiated photoplay criticism. That is a big thing to have done, and he has done it, to use his own style, with Action, Intimacy, and Friendliness, and Splendor." The statement is still true; and I'm happy that this book, so long neglected, is available again.

A WORD FROM THE DIRECTOR
OF THE DENVER ART ASSOCIATION

The Art of the Moving Picture, as it appeared six years ago, possessed among many elements of beauty at least one peculiarity. It viewed art as a reality, and one of our most familiar and popular realities as an art. This should have made the book either a revelation or utter Greek to most of us, and those who read it probably dropped it easily into one or the other of the two categories.

For myself, long a propagandist for its doctrines in another but related field, the book came as a great solace. In it I found, not an appeal to have the art museum used — which would have been an old though welcome story — not this, but much to my surprise, the art museum actually at work, one of the very wheels on which our culture rolled forward upon its hopeful way. I saw among other museums the one whose destinies I was tenderly guiding, playing in Lindsay's book the part that is played by the classic myths in Milton, or by the dictionary in the writings of the rest of us. For once the museum and its contents appeared, not as a lovely curiosity, but as one of the basic, and in a sense humble necessities of life. To paraphrase the author's own text, the art museum, like the furniture in a good movie, was actually "in motion" — a character in the play. On this point of view as on a pivot turns the whole book.

In The Art of the Moving Picture the nature and domain of a new Muse is defined. She is the first legitimate addition to the family since classic times. And as it required trained painters of pictures like Fulton and Morse to visualize the possibility of the steamboat and the telegraph, so the bold seer who perceived the true nature of this new star in our nightly heavens, it should here be recorded, acquired much of the vision of his seeing eye through an early training in art. Vachel Lindsay (as he himself proudly asserts) was a student at the Institute in Chicago for four years, spent one more at the League and at Chase's in New York, and for four more haunted the Metropolitan Museum, lecturing to his fellows on every art there shown from the Egyptian to that of Arthur B. Davies.

Only such a background as this could have

evolved the conception of "Architecture, sculpture, and painting in motion" and given authenticity to its presentation. The validity of Lindsay's analysis is attested by Freeburg's helpful characterization, "Composition in fluid forms," which it seems to have suggested. To Lindsay's category one would be tempted to add, "pattern in motion," applying it to such a film as the "Caligari" which he and I have seen together and discussed during these past few days. Pattern in this connection would imply an emphasis on the intrinsic suggestion of the spot and shape apart from their immediate relation to the appearance of natural objects. But this is a digression. It simply serves to show the breadth and adaptability of Lindsay's method.

The book was written for a visual-minded public and for those who would be its leaders. A long, long line of picture-readers trailing from the dawn of history, stimulated all the masterpieces of pictorial art from Altamira to Michelangelo. For less than five centuries now Gutenberg has had them scurrying to learn their A, B, C's, but they are drifting back to their old ways again, and nightly are forming themselves in cues at the doorways of the

"Isis," the "Tivoli," and the "Riviera," the while it is sadly noted that "'the pictures' are driving literature off the parlor table."

With the creative implications of this new pictorial art, with the whole visual-minded race clamoring for more, what may we not dream in the way of a new renaissance? How are we to step in to the possession of such a destiny? Are the institutions with a purely literary theory of life going to meet the need? Are the art schools and the art museums making themselves ready to assimilate a new art form? Or what is the type of institution that will ultimately take the position of leadership in culture through this new universal instrument?

What possibilities lie in this art, once it is understood and developed, to plant new conceptions of civic and national idealism? How far may it go in cultivating concerted emotion in the now ungoverned crowd? Such questions as these can be answered only by minds with the imagination to see art as a reality; with faith to visualize for the little mid-western "home town" a new and living Pallas Athena; with courage to raze the very houses of the city to make new and greater forums and "civic centres."

For ourselves in Denver, we shall try to do justice to the new Muse. In the museum which we build we shall provide a shrine for her. We shall first endeavor by those simple means which lie to our hands, to know the areas of charm and imagination which remain as yet an untilled field of her domain. Plowing is a simple art, but it requires much sweat. This at least we know — to the expenditure we cheerfully consent. So much for the beginning. It would be boastful to describe plans to keep pace with the enlarging of the motion picture field before a real beginning is made. But with youth in its favor, the Denver Art Museum hopes yet to see this art set in its rightful place with painting, sculpture, architecture, and the handicrafts — hopes yet to be an instrument in the great work of making this art real as those others are being even now made real, to the expanding vision of an eager people.

GEORGE WILLIAM EGGERS

DENVER, COLORADO,
New Year's Day, 1922.

Director
The Denver Art Association

THE ART OF
THE MOVING PICTURE

BOOK I — THE GENERAL PHOTOPLAY SITUATION IN AMERICA, JANUARY 1, 1922

Especially as Viewed from the Heights of the Civic Centre at Denver, Colorado, and the Denver Art Museum, Which Is to Be a Leading Feature of This Civic Centre

In the second chapter of book two, on page 8, the theoretical outline begins, with a discussion of the Photoplay of Action. I put there on record the first crude commercial films that in any way establish the principle. There can never be but one first of anything, and if the negatives of these films survive the shrinking and the warping that comes with time, they will still be, in a certain sense, classic, and ten years hence or two years hence will still be better remembered than any films of the current releases, which come on like newspapers, and as George Ade says: — "Nothing is so dead as yesterday's newspaper." But the first newspapers, and the first imprints of Addison's Spectator, and the first Almanacs of Benjamin Franklin, and the first broadside ballads and the like, are ever collected and remembered. And the lists of films given in books two and three of this work are the only critical and carefully sorted lists of the early motion pictures that I happen to know anything about. I hope to be corrected if I am too boastful, but I boast that my lists must be referred to by all those who desire to study these experiments in their beginnings. So I let them remain, as still vivid in the memory of all true lovers of the photoplay who have watched its growth, fascinated from the first. But I would add to the list of Action Films of chapter two the recent popular example, Douglas Fairbanks in The Three Musketeers. That is perhaps the most literal "Chase-Picture" that was ever really successful in the commercial world. The story is cut to one episode. The whole task of the four famous swordsmen of Dumas is to get the Queen's token that is in the hands of Buckingham in England, and return with it to Paris in time for the great ball. It is one long race with the Cardinal's guards who are at last left behind. It is the same plot as Reynard the Fox, John Masefield's poem — Reynard successfully eluding the huntsmen and the dogs. If that poem is ever put on in an Art Museum film, it will have to be staged like one of Æsop's Fables, with a *man* acting the Fox, for the children's delight. And I earnestly urge all who would understand the deeper significance of the "chase-picture" or the "Action Picture" to give more thought to Masefield's poem than to Fairbanks' marvellous acting in the school of the younger Salvini. The Mood of the *intimate photoplay*, chapter three, still remains indicated in the current films by the acting of Lillian Gish and Mary Pickford, when they are not roused up by their directors to turn handsprings to keep the people staring. Mary Pickford in particular has been stimulated to be over-athletic, and in all her career she has been given just one chance to be her more delicate self, and that was in the almost forgotten film : — A Romance of the Redwoods. This is one of the serious commercial attempts that should be revived and studied, in spite of its crudities of plot, by our Art Museums. There is something of the grandeur of the redwoods in it, in contrast to the sustained Botticelli grace of "Our Mary."

I am the one poet who has a right to claim

for his muses Blanche Sweet, Mary Pickford, and Mae Marsh. I am the one poet who wrote them songs when they were Biograph heroines, before their names were put on the screen, or the name of their director. Woman's clubs are always asking me for bits of delicious gossip about myself to fill up literary essays. Now there's a bit. There are two things to be said for those poems. First, they were heartfelt. Second, any one could improve on them.

In the fourth chapter of book two I discourse elaborately and formally on The Motion Picture of Fairy Splendor. And to this carefully balanced technical discourse I would add the informal word, this New Year's Day, that this type is best illustrated by such fairy-tales as have been most ingratiatingly retold in the books of Padraic Colum, and dazzlingly illustrated by Willy Pogany. The Colum-Pogany School of Thought is one which the commercial producers have not yet condescended to illustrate in celluloid, and it remains a special province for the Art Museum Film. Fairy-tales need not be more than one-tenth of a reel long. Some of the best fairy-tales in the whole history of man can be told in a breath. And the best motion picture story for fifty years may turn out to be a reel ten minutes long. Do not let the length of the commercial film tyrannize over your mind, O young art museum photoplay director. Remember the brevity of Lincoln's Gettysburg address. . . .

And so my commentary, New Year's Day, 1922, proceeds, using for points of more and more extensive departure the refrains and old catch-phrases of books two and three.

Chapter V — The Picture of Crowd Splendor, being the type illustrated by Griffith's Intolerance.

Chapter VI — The Picture of Patriotic Splendor, which was illustrated by all the War Films, the one most recently approved and accepted by the public being The Four Horsemen of the Apocalypse.

Chapter VII — The Picture of Religious Splendor, which has no examples, that remain in the memory with any sharpness in 1922, except The Faith Healer, founded on the play by William Vaughn Moody, the poet, with much of the directing and scenario by Mrs. William Vaughn Moody, and a more talked-of commercial film, The Miracle Man.

But not until the religious film is taken out of the commercial field, and allowed to develop unhampered under the Church and the Art Museum, will the splendid religious and ritualistic opportunity be realized.

Chapter VIII — Sculpture-in-Motion, being a continuation of the argument of chapter two, The Photoplay of Action. Like the Action Film, this aspect of composition is much better understood by the commercial people than some other sides of the art. Some of the best of the William S. Hart productions show appreciation of this quality by the director, the photographer, and the public. Not only is the man but the horse allowed to be moving bronze, and not mere cowboy pasteboard. Many of the pictures of Charles Ray make the hero quite a bronze-looking sculpturesque person, despite his yokel raiment.

Chapter   IX — Painting-in-Motion, being a continuation on a higher terrace of chapter three, The Intimate Photoplay. Charlie Chaplin has intimate and painter's qualities in his acting, and he makes himself into a painting or an etching in the midst of furious slapstick. But he has been in no films that were themselves paintings. The argument of this chapter has been carried much further in Freeburg's book, The Art of Photoplay Making.

Chapter X — Furniture, Trappings, and Inventions in Motion, being a continuation of the chapter on Fairy Splendor. In this field we find one of the worst failures of the commercial films, and their utterly unimaginative corporation promoters. Again I must refer them to such fairy books as those of Padraic Colum, where neither sword nor wing nor boat is found to move, except for a fairy reason.

I have just returned this very afternoon from a special showing of the famous imported film, The Cabinet of Dr. Caligari. Some of the earnest spirits of the Denver Art Association, finding it was in storage in the town, had it privately brought forth to study it with reference to its bearing on their new policies. What influence it will have in that most vital group, time will show.

Meanwhile it is a marvellous illustration of the meaning of this chapter and the chapter on Fairy Splendor, though it is a diabolical not a beneficent vitality that is given to inanimate things. The furniture, trappings, and inventions are in motion to express the haunted mind, as in Griffith's Avenging Conscience, described pages 121 through 132. The two should be shown together in the same afternoon, in the Art Museum study rooms. Caligari is undoubtedly the most important imported film since that work of D'Annunzio, Cabiria, described pages 55 through 57. But it is the opposite type of film. Cabiria is all out-doors and splendor on the Mediterranean scale. In general, imported films do not concern Americans, for we have now a vast range of technique. All we lack is the sense to use it.

The cabinet of Caligari is indeed a cabinet, and the feeling of being in a cell, and smothered by all the oppressions of a weary mind, does not desert the spectator for a minute.

The play is more important, technically, than in its subject-matter and mood. It proves in a hundred new ways the resources of the film in making all the inanimate things which, on the spoken stage, cannot act at all, the leading actors in the films. But they need not necessarily act to a diabolical end. An angel could have as well been brought from the cabinet as a murderous somnambulist, and every act of his could have been a work of beneficence and health and healing. I

could not help but think that the ancient
miracle play of the resurrection of Osiris could
have been acted out with similar simple means,
with a mummy case and great sarcophagus.
The wings of Isis and Nephthys could have
been spread over the sky instead of the oppressive walls of the crooked city. Lights
instead of shadows could have been made
actors and real hieroglyphic inscriptions instead of scrawls.

As it was, the alleged insane man was more
sensible than most motion picture directors,
for his scenery acted with him, and not according to accident or silly formula. I make
these points as an antidote to the general
description of this production by those who
praise it.

They speak of the scenery as grotesque,
strained, and experimental, and the plot as
sinister. But this does not get to the root of
the matter. There is rather the implication
in most of the criticisms and praises that the
scenery is abstract. Quite the contrary is
the case. Indoors looks like indoors. Streets
are always streets, roofs are always roofs.
The actors do not move about in a kind of
crazy geometry as I was led to believe. The

scenery is oppressive, but sane, and the obsession is for the most part expressed in the acting and plot. The fair looks like a fair and the library looks like a library. There is nothing experimental about any of the setting, nothing unconsidered or strained or over-considered. It seems experimental because it is thrown into contrast with extreme commercial formulas in the regular line of the "movie trade." But compare The Cabinet of Dr. Caligari with a book of Rackham or Du Lac or Dürer, or Rembrandt's etchings, and Dr. Caligari is more realistic. And Eggers insists the whole film is replete with suggestions of the work of Pieter Breughel, the painter. Hundreds of indoor stories will be along such lines, once the merely commercial motive is eliminated, and the artist is set free. This film is an extraordinary variation of the intimate, as expounded in chapter three. It is drawing-in-motion, instead of painting-in-motion. Because it was drawing instead of painting, literary-minded people stepped to the hasty conclusion it was experimental. Half-tone effects are, for the most part, eliminated. Line is dominant everywhere. It is the opposite of vast conceptions like Theodora — which are architecture-in-motion. All the architecture of the Caligari film seems paste-board. The whole thing happens in a cabinet.

It is the most overwhelming contrast to Griffith's Intolerance that could be in any way imagined. It contains, one may say, all the effects left out of Intolerance. The word cabinet is a quadruple pun. Not only does it mean a mystery box and a box holding a somnambulist, but a kind of treasury of tiny twisted thoughts. There is not one line or conception in it on the grand scale, or even the grandiose. It is a devil's toy-house. One feels like a mouse in a mouse-trap so small one cannot turn around. In Intolerance, Griffith hurls nation at nation, race at race, century against century, and his camera is not only a telescope across the plains of Babylon, but across the ages. Griffith is, in Intolerance, the ungrammatical Byron of the films, but certainly as magnificent as Byron, and since he is the first of his kind I, for one, am willing to name him with Marlowe.

But for technical study for Art Schools, The Cabinet of Dr. Caligari is more profitable. It shows how masterpieces can be made, with the second-hand furniture of any attic. But I hope fairy-tales, not diabolical stories, will come from these attics. Fairy-tales are inherent in the genius of the motion picture and are a thousand times hinted at in the commercial films, though the commercial films are not willing to stop to tell them. Lillian Gish could be given wings and a wand if she only had directors and scenario writers who believed in fairies. And the same can most heartily be said of Mae Marsh.

Chapter XI — Architecture-in-Motion, being a continuation of the argument about the Splendor Pictures, in chapters five, six, and seven. This is an element constantly re-illustrated in a magnificent but fragmentary way by the News Films. Any picture of a sea-gull flying so close to the camera that it becomes as large as a flying machine, or any flying machine made by man and photographed in epic flight captures the eye because it is architecture and in motion, motion which is the mysterious fourth dimension of its grace and glory. So likewise, and in kind, any picture of a tossing ship. The most superb example of architecture-in-motion in the commercial history of the films is the march of the moving war-towers against the walls of Babylon in Griffith's Intolerance. But Griffith is the only person so far who has known how to put a fighting soul into a moving tower.

The only real war that has occurred in the films with the world's greatest war going on outside was Griffith's War Against Babylon. The rest was news.

Chapter XII — Thirty Differences between the Photoplays and the Stage. The argument of the whole of the 1915 edition has been accepted by the studios, the motion picture magazines, and the daily motion picture columns throughout the land. I have read hundreds of editorials and magazines, and scarcely one that differed from it in theory. Most of them read like paraphrases of this work. And of all arguments made, the one in this chapter is the one oftenest accepted in its entirety. The people who dominate the films are obviously those who grew up with them from the very beginning, and the merely stage actors who rushed in with the highest tide of prosperity now have to take second rank if they remain in the films. But most of these have gone back to the stage by this time, with their managers as well, and certainly this chapter is abundantly proved out.

Chapter XIII — Hieroglyphics.   One of

the implications of this chapter and the one preceding is that the fewer words printed on the screen the better, and that the ideal film has no words printed on it at all, but is one unbroken sheet of photography. This is admitted in theory in all the studios now, though the only film of the kind ever produced of general popular success was The Old Swimmin' Hole, acted by Charles Ray. If I remember, there was not one word on the screen, after the cast of characters was given. The whole story was clearly and beautifully told by Photoplay Hieroglyphics. For this feature alone, despite many defects of the film, it should be studied in every art school in America.

Meanwhile "Title writing" remains a commercial necessity. In this field there is but one person who has won distinction — Anita Loos. She is one of the four or five important and thoroughly artistic brains in the photoplay game. Among them is the distinguished John Emerson. In combination with John Emerson, director, producer, etc., she has done so many other things well, her talents as a title writer are incidental, but certainly to be mentioned in this place.

The outline we are discussing continues through

Book III — More Personal Speculations and Afterthoughts Not Brought Forward so Dogmatically.

Chapter XIV — The Orchestra, Conversation, and the Censorship. In this chapter, on page 189, I suggest suppressing the orchestra entirely and encouraging the audience to talk about the film. No photoplay people have risen to contradict this theory, but it is a chapter that once caused me great embarrassment. With Christopher Morley, the well-known author of Shandygaff and other temperance literature, I was trying to prove out this chapter. As soon as the orchestra stopped, while the show rolled on in glory, I talked about the main points in this book, illustrating it by the film before us. Almost everything that happened was a happy illustration of my ideas. But there were two shop girls in front of us awfully in love with a certain second-rate actor who insisted on kissing the heroine every so often, and with her apparent approval. Every time we talked about that those shop girls glared at us as though we were robbing them of their time and money. Finally one of them dragged

the other out into the aisle, and dashed out
of the house with her dear chum, saying, so
all could hear: "Well, come on, Terasa, we
might as well go, if these two talking *pests* are
going to keep this up behind us." The poor
girl's voice trembled. She was in tears. She
was gone before we could apologize or offer
flowers. So I say in applying this chapter,
in our present stage of civilization, sit on the
front seat, where no one can hear your whisper-
ings but Mary Pickford on the screen. She is
but a shadow there, and will not mind.

Chapter XV — The Substitute for the Saloon.
I leave this argument as a monument, just
as it was written, in 1914 and '15. It indicates
a certain power of forecasting on the part of
the writer. We drys have certainly won a
great victory. Some of the photoplay people
agree with this temperance sermon, and
some of them do not. The wets make one
mistake above all. They do not realize that
the drys can still keep on voting dry, with
intense conviction, and great battle cries, and
still have a sense of humor.

Chapter XVI — California and America.
This chapter was quoted and paraphrased
almost bodily as the preface to my volume of

verses, The Golden Whales of California. "I Know All This When Gipsy Fiddles Cry," a song of some length recently published in the New Republic and the London Nation, further expresses the sentiment of this chapter in what I hope is a fraternal way, and I hope suggests the day when California will have power over India, Asia, and all the world, and plant giant redwood trees of the spirit the world around.

Chapter XVII — Progress and Endowment. I allow this discourse, also, to stand as written in 1914 and '15. It shows the condition just before the war, better than any new words of mine could do it. The main change now is the growing hope of a backing, not only from Universities, but great Art Museums.

Chapter XVIII — Architects as Crusaders. The sermon in this chapter has been carried out on a limited scale, and as a result of the suggestion, or from pure American instinct, we now have handsome gasoline filling stations from one end of America to the other, and really gorgeous Ford garages. Our Union depots and our magazine stands in the leading hotels, and our big Soda fountains are more and more attractive all the time. Having recited of late about twice around the United

States and, continuing the pilgrimage, I can
testify that they are all alike from New York
to San Francisco.   One has to ask the hotel
clerk to find out whether it is New York or
———.   And the motion picture discipline of the
American eye has had a deal to do with this
increasing tendency to news-stand and architectural   standardization   and   architectural
thinking, such as it is.   But I meant this
suggestion to go further, and to be taken in a
higher sense, so I ask these people to read this
chapter again.   I have carried out the idea,
in   a   parable,   perhaps   more   clearly   in   The
Golden Book of Springfield, when I speak of
the World's Fair of the University of Springfield, to be built one hundred years hence.   And
I would recommend to those who have already
taken seriously chapter eighteen, to re-read it in
two towns, amply worth the car fare it costs
to go to both of them.   First, Santa Fe, New
Mexico, at the end of the Santa Fe Trail, the
oldest city in the United States, the richest in
living traditions, and with the oldest and the
newest architecture in the United States; not
a stone or a stick of it standardized, a city with
a soul, Jerusalem and Mecca and Benares and
Thebes for any artist or any poet of America's

future, or any one who would dream of great cities born of great architectural photoplays, or great photoplays born of great cities. And the other city, symbolized by The Golden Rain Tree in The Golden Book of Springfield, is New Harmony, Indiana. That was the Greenwich Village of America more than one hundred years ago, when it was yet in the heart of the wilderness, millions of miles from the sea. It has a tradition already as dusty and wonderful as Abydos and Gem Aten. And every stone is still eloquent of individualism, and standardization has not yet set its foot there. Is it not possible for the architects to brood in such places and then say to one another : — "Build from your hearts buildings and films which shall be your individual Hieroglyphics, each according to his own loves and fancies?"

Chapter XIX — On Coming Forth by Day. This is the second Egyptian chapter. It has its direct relation to the Hieroglyphic chapter, page 171. I note that I say here it costs a dime to go to the show. Well, now it costs around thirty cents to go to a good show in a respectable suburb, sometimes fifty cents. But we will let that dime remain there, as a matter of historic interest, and pass on, to higher themes.

Certainly the Hieroglyphic chapter is in words of one syllable and any kindergarten teacher can understand it. Chapter nineteen adds a bit to the idea. I do not know how warranted I am in displaying Egyptian learning. Newspaper reporters never tire of getting me to talk about hieroglyphics in their relation to the photoplays, and always give me respectful headlines on the theme. I can only say that up to this hour, every time I have toured art museums, I have begun with the Egyptian exhibit, and if my patient guest was willing, lectured on every period on to the present time, giving a little time to the principal exhibits in each room, but I have always found myself returning to Egypt as a standard. It seems my natural classic land of art. So when I took up hieroglyphics more seriously last summer, I found them extraordinarily easy as though I were looking at a "movie" in a book. I think Egyptian picture-writing came easy because I have analyzed so many hundreds of photoplay films, merely for recreation, and the same style of composition is in both. Any child who reads one can read the other. But

of course the literal translation must be there
at hand to correct all wrong guesses. I figure
that in just one thousand years I can read
hieroglyphics without a pony. But meanwhile, I tour museums and I ride Pharaoh's
"horse," and suggest to all photoplay enthusiasts they do the same. I recommend these
two books most heartily : Elementary Egyptian
Grammar, by Margaret A. Murray, London,
Bernard Quaritch, 11 Grafton Street, Bond
Street, W., dnd the three volumes of the
Book of the Dead, which are, indeed, the
Papyrus of Ani, referred to in this chapter,
pages 255–258. It is edited, translated, and
reproduced in fac-simile by the keeper of the
Egyptian and Assyrian Antiquities in the
British Museum, Professor E. A. Wallis Budge ;
published by G. P. Putnam's Sons, New York,
and Philip Lee Warner, London. This book
is certainly the greatest motion picture I ever
attended. I have gone through it several times,
and it is the only book one can read twelve
hours at a stretch, on the Pullman, when he is
making thirty-six hour and forty-eight hour
jumps from town to town.

American civilization grows more hieroglyphic every day. The cartoons of Darling,

the advertisements in the back of the magazines
and on the bill-boards and in the street-cars,
the acres of photographs in the Sunday newspapers, make us into a hieroglyphic civilization
far nearer to Egypt than to England. Let
us then accept for our classic land, for our
standard of form, the country naturally our
own.   Hieroglyphics are so much nearer to the
American mood than the rest of the Egyptian
legacy, that Americans seldom get as far as
the Hieroglyphics to discover how congenial
they are.   Seeing the mummies, good Americans
flee.   But there is not a man in America writing
advertisements or making cartoons or films
but would find delightful the standard books
of Hieroglyphics sent out by the British
Museum, once he gave them a chance.   They
represent that very aspect of visual life which
Europe understands so little in America, and
which has been expanding so enormously even
the last year.   Hallowe'en, for instance, lasts
a whole week now, with mummers on the
streets every night, October 25–31.

Chapter XX — The Prophet-Wizard.   Who
do we mean by The Prophet-Wizard?   We
mean not only artists, such as are named in
this chapter, but dreamers and workers like

Johnny Appleseed, or Abraham Lincoln. The best account of Johnny Appleseed is in Harper's Monthly for November, 1871. People do not know Abraham Lincoln till they have visited the grave of Anne Rutledge, at Petersburg, Illinois, then New Old Salem a mile away. New Old Salem is a prophet's hill, on the edge of the Sangamon, with lovely woods all around. Here a brooding soul could be born, and here the dreamer Abraham Lincoln spent his real youth. I do not call him a dreamer in a cheap and sentimental effort to describe a man of aspiration. Lincoln told and interpreted his visions like Joseph and Daniel in the Old Testament, revealing them to the members of his cabinet, in great trials of the Civil War. People who do not see visions and dream dreams in the good Old Testament sense have no right to leadership in America. I would prefer photoplays filled with such visions and oracles to the state papers written by "practical men." As it is, we are ruled indirectly by photoplays owned and controlled by men who should be in the shoe-string and hook-and-eye trade. Apparently their digestions are good, they are in excellent health, and they keep out of jail.

Chapter XXI — The Acceptable Year of the Lord. If I may be pardoned for referring again to the same book, I assumed, in The Golden Book of Springfield, Illinois, that the Acceptable Year of the Lord would come for my city beginning November 1, 2018, and that up to that time, amid much of joy, there would also be much of thwarting and tribulation. But in the beginning of that mystic November, the Soul of My City, named Avanel, would become as much a part of the city as Pallas Athena was Athens, and indeed I wrote into the book much of the spirit of the photoplay outlined, pages 147 through 150. But in The Golden Book I changed the lady the city worshipped from a golden image into a living, breathing young girl, descendant of that great American, Daniel Boone, and her name, obviously, Avanel Boone. With her tribe she incarnates all the mystic ideals of the Boones of Kentucky.

All this but a prelude to saying that I have just passed through the city of Santa Fe, New Mexico. It is a Santa Fe full of the glory of the New Architecture of which I have spoken, and the issuing of a book of cowboy songs collected, and many of them written, by

N. Howard Thorp, a citizen of Santa Fe, and thrilling with the issuing of a book of poems about the Glory of New Mexico. This book is called Red Earth. It is by Alice Corbin Henderson. And Santa Fe is full of the glory of a magnificent State Capitol that is an art gallery of the whole southwest, and the glories of the studio of William Penhallow Henderson, who has painted our New Arabia more splendidly than it was ever painted before, with the real character thereof, and no theatricals. This is just the kind of a town I hoped for when I wrote my first draft of The Art of the Moving Picture. Here now is literature and art. When they become one art as of old in Egypt, we will have New Mexico Hieroglyphics from the Hendersons and their kind, and their surrounding Indian pupils, a basis for the American Motion Picture more acceptable, and more patriotic, and more organic for us than the Egyptian.

And I come the same month to Denver, and find a New Art Museum projected, which I hope has much indeed to do with the Acceptable Year of the Lord, when films as vital as the Santa Fe songs and pictures and architecture can be made, and in common spirit with them,

in this New Arabia. George W. Eggers, the
director of the newly projected Denver Art
Museum, assures me that a photoplay policy
can be formulated, amid the problems of such
an all around undertaking as building a great
Art Museum in Denver. He expects to give
the photoplay the attention a new art deserves,
especially when it affects almost every person
in the whole country. So I prophesy Denver
to be the Museum and Art-school capital of
New Arabia, as Santa Fe is the artistic, architectural, and song capital at this hour. And
I hope it may become the motion picture
capital of America from the standpoint of pure
art, not manufacture.

What do I mean by New Arabia?

When I was in London in the fall of 1920 the
editor of The Landmark, the organ of The
English Speaking Union, asked me to draw my
map of the United States. I marked out the
various regions under various names. For
instance I called the coast states, Washington,
Oregon, and California, New Italy. The reasons
may be found in the chapter in this book
on California. Then I named the states just
west of the Middle West, and east of New Italy,
New Arabia. These states are New Mexico,

Arizona, Utah, Colorado, Wyoming, Idaho, and Montana. These are the states which carry the Rocky Mountains north toward the Aurora Borealis, and south toward the tropics. Here individualism, Andrew Jacksonism, will forever prevail, and American standardization can never prevail. In cabins that cannot be reached by automobile and deserts that cannot be crossed by boulevards, the John the Baptists, the hermits and the prophets can strengthen their souls. Here are lonely places as sweet for the spirit as was little old New Salem, Illinois, one hundred years ago, or the wilderness in which walked Johnny Appleseed.

Now it is the independence of Spirit of this New Arabia that I hope the Denver Art Museum can interpret in its photoplay films, and send them on circuits to the Art Museums springing up all over America, where sculpture, architecture, and painting are now constantly sent on circuit. Let that already established convention — the "circuit-exhibition" — be applied to this new art.

And after Denver has shown the way, I devoutly hope that Great City of Los Angeles may follow her example. Consider, O Great City of Los Angeles, now almost the equal of

New York in power and splendor, consider what it would do for the souls of all your film artists if you projected just such a museum as Denver is now projecting. Your fate is coming toward you. Denver is halfway between Chicago, with the greatest art institute in the country, and Los Angeles, the natural capital of the photoplay. The art museums of America should rule the universities, and the photoplay studios as well. In the art museums should be set the final standards of civic life, rather than in any musty libraries or routine classrooms. And the great weapon of the art museums of all the land should be the hieroglyphic of the future, the truly artistic photoplay.

And now for book two, at length. It is a detailed analysis of the films, first proclaimed in 1915, and never challenged or overthrown, and, for the most part, accepted intact by the photoplay people, and the critics and the theorists, as well.

BOOK II — THE UNCHALLENGED OUTLINE OF PHOTOPLAY CRITICAL METHOD

CHAPTER I

THE POINT OF VIEW

WHILE there is a great deal of literary reference in all the following argument, I realize, looking back over many attempts to paraphrase it for various audiences, that its appeal is to those who spend the best part of their student life in classifying, and judging, and producing works of sculpture, painting, and architecture. I find the eyes of all others wandering when I make talks upon the plastic artist's point of view.

This book tries to find that fourth dimension of architecture, painting, and sculpture, which is the human soul in action, that arrow with wings which is the flash of fire from the film, or the heart of man, or Pygmalion's image, when it becomes a woman.

The 1915 edition was used by Victor O. Freeburg as one of the text-books in the Columbia University School of Journalism, in his classes in photoplay writing. I was invited several times to address those classes on my yearly visits to New York. I have addressed many other academic classes, the invitation being based on this book. Now I realize that those who approach the theory from the general University standpoint, or from the history of the drama, had best begin with Freeburg's book, for he is not only learned in both matters, but presents the special analogies with skill. Freeburg has an excellent education in the history of music, and some of the happiest passages in his work relate the photoplay to the musical theory of the world, as my book relates it to the general Art Museum point of view of the world. Emphatically, my book belongs in the Art Institutes as a beginning, or in such religious and civic bodies as think architecturally. From there it must work its way out. Of course those bodies touch on a thousand others.

The work is being used as one basis of the campaign for the New Denver Art Museum, and I like to tell the story of how George W.

Eggers of Denver first began to apply the book
when the Director of the Art Institute, Chicago,
that it may not seem to the merely University
type of mind a work of lost abstractions. One
of the most gratifying recognitions I ever
received was the invitation to talk on the films
in Fullerton Hall, Chicago Art Institute.
Then there came invitations to speak at
Chicago University, and before the Fort-
nightly Club, Chicago, all around 1916–17.
One difficulty was getting the film to *prove*
my case from out the commercial whirl. I
talked at these three and other places, but
hardly knew how to go about crossing the
commercial bridge. At last, with the co-
operation of Director Eggers, we staged, in the
sacred precincts of Fullerton Hall, Mae Marsh
in The Wild Girl of the Sierras. The film was
in battered condition, and was turned so fast
I could not talk with it satisfactorily and fulfil
the well-known principles of chapter fourteen.
But at least I had converted one Art Institute
Director to the idea that an ex-student of the
Institute could not only write a book about
painting-in-motion, but the painting could be
shown in an Art Museum as promise of greater
things in this world. It took a deal of will

and breaking of precedent, on the part of all
concerned, to show this film, The Wild Girl of
the Sierras, and I retired from the field a long
time. But now this same Eggers is starting, in
Denver, an Art Museum from its very foundations, but on the same constructive scale.
So this enterprise, in my fond and fatuous
fancy, is associated with the sweet Mae Marsh
as The Wild Girl of the Sierras — one of the
loveliest bits of poetry ever put into screen or
fable.

For about one year, off and on, I had the
honor to be the photoplay critic of The New
Republic, this invitation also based on the
first edition of this book. Looking back upon
that experience I am delighted to affirm that
not only The New Republic constituency but
the world of the college and the university where
I moved at that time, while at loss for a policy,
were not only willing but eager to take the
films with seriousness.

But when I was through with all these
dashes into the field, and went back to reciting
verses again, no one had given me any light
as to who should make the disinterested, non-
commercial film for these immediate times,
the film that would class, in our civilization, with

The New Republic or The Atlantic Monthly
or the poems of Edwin Arlington Robinson.
That is, the production not for the trade, but
for the soul. Anita Loos, that good crusader,
came out several years ago with the flaming
announcement that there was now hope, since
a school of films had been heavily endowed
for the University of Rochester. The school
was to be largely devoted to producing music
for the photoplay, in defiance of chapter
fourteen. But incidentally there were to
be motion pictures made to fit good music.
Neither music nor films have as yet shaken
the world.

I liked this Rochester idea. I felt that once
it was started the films would take their proper
place and dominate the project, disinterested
non-commercial films to be classed with the
dramas so well stimulated by the great
drama department under Professor Baker of
Harvard.

As I look back over this history I see that
the printed page had counted too much, and
the real forces of the visible arts in America
had not been definitely enlisted. They should
take the lead. I would suggest as the three
people to interview first on building any Art

Museum Photoplay project: Victor Freeburg, with his long experience of teaching the
subject in Columbia, and John Emerson and
Anita Loos, who are as brainy as people dare
to be and still remain in the department store
film business. No three people would more
welcome opportunities to outline the idealistic
possibilities of this future art. And a well-known
American painter was talking to me of a midnight scolding Charlie Chaplin gave to some Los
Angeles producer, in a little restaurant, preach-
ing the really beautiful film, and denouncing
commerce like a member of Coxey's illustrious
army. And I have heard rumors from all sides
that Charlie Chaplin has a soul. He is the
comedian most often proclaimed an artist by
the fastidious, and most often forgiven for
his slapstick. He is praised for a kind of
O. Henry double meaning to his antics. He is
said to be like one of O. Henry's misquotations
of the classics. He looks to me like that artist
Edgar Poe, if Poe had been obliged to make
millions laugh. I do not like Chaplin's work,
but I have to admit the good intentions and
the enviable laurels. Let all the Art Museums
invite him in, as tentative adviser, if not a
chastened performer. Let him be given as

good a chance as Mae Marsh was given by Eggers in Fullerton Hall. Only let him come in person, not in film, till we hear him speak, and consider his suggestions, and make sure he has eaten of the mystic Amaranth Apples of Johnny Appleseed.

CHAPTER II

THE PHOTOPLAY OF ACTION

LET us assume, friendly reader, that it is eight o'clock in the evening when you make yourself comfortable in your den, to peruse this chapter. I want to tell you about the Action Film, the simplest, the type most often seen. In the mind of the habitué of the cheaper theatre it is the only sort in existence. It dominates the slums, is announced there by red and green posters of the melodrama sort, and retains its original elements, more deftly handled, in places more expensive. The story goes at the highest possible speed to be still credible. When it is a poor thing, which is the case too often, the St. Vitus dance destroys the pleasure-value. The rhythmic quality of the picture-motions is twitched to death. In the bad photoplay even the picture of an express train more than exaggerates itself. Yet when the photoplay chooses to behave it can reproduce a race far more joyously than the stage. On that fact is based the opportunity

of this form. Many Action Pictures are indoors, but the abstract theory of the Action
Film is based on the out-of-door chase. You
remember the first one you saw where the
policeman pursues the comical tramp over
hill and dale and across the town lots. You
remember that other where the cowboy follows
the horse thief across the desert, spies him at
last and chases him faster, faster, faster, and
faster, and finally catches him. If the film
was made in the days before the National
Board of Censorship, it ends with the cowboy
cheerfully hanging the villain; all details given
to the last kick of the deceased.

One of the best Action Pictures is an old
Griffith Biograph, recently reissued, the story
entitled "Man's Genesis." In the time when
cave-men-gorillas had no weapons, Weak-
Hands (impersonated by Robert Harron)
invents the stone club. He vanquishes his
gorilla-like rival, Brute-Force (impersonated
by Wilfred Lucas). Strange but credible manners and customs of the cave-men are detailed.
They live in picturesque caves. Their half-
monkey gestures are wonderful to see. But
these things are beheld on the fly. It is the
chronicle of a race between the brain of Weak-

Hands and the body of the other, symbolized by the chasing of poor Weak-Hands in and out among the rocks until the climax. Brain desperately triumphs. Weak-Hands slays Brute-Force with the startling invention. He wins back his stolen bride, Lily-White (impersonated by Mae Marsh). It is a Griffith masterpiece, and every actor does sound work. The audience, mechanical Americans, fond of crawling on their stomachs to tinker their automobiles, are eager over the evolution of the first weapon from a stick to a hammer. They are as full of curiosity as they could well be over the history of Langley or the Wright brothers.

The dire perils of the motion pictures provoke the ingenuity of the audience, not their passionate sympathy. When, in the minds of the deluded producers, the beholders should be weeping or sighing with desire, they are prophesying the next step to one another in worldly George Ade slang. This is illustrated in another good Action Photoplay: the dramatization of The Spoilers. The original novel was written by Rex Beach. The gallant William Farnum as Glenister dominates the play. He has excellent support. Their team-work makes them worthy of chronicle: Thomas Santschi as

McNamara, Kathlyn Williams as Cherry Ma-
lotte, Bessie Eyton as Helen Chester, Frank
Clark as Dextry, Wheeler Oakman as Bronco
Kid, and Jack McDonald as Slapjack.

There are, in The Spoilers, inspiriting ocean
scenes and mountain views. There are interesting sketches of mining-camp manners
and customs. There is a well-acted love-
interest in it, and the element of the comradeship of loyal pals. But the chase rushes past
these things to the climax, as in a policeman
picture it whirls past blossoming gardens and
front lawns till the tramp is arrested. The
difficulties are commented on by the people
in the audience as rah-rah boys on the side
lines comment on hurdles cleared or knocked
over by the men running in college field-day.
The sudden cut-backs into side branches of the
story are but hurdles also, not plot complica-
tions in the stage sense. This is as it should be.
The pursuit progresses without St. Vitus dance
or hysteria to the end of the film. There the
spoilers are discomfited, the gold mine is re-
captured, the incidental girls are won, in a
flash, by the rightful owners.

These shows work like the express elevators
in the Metropolitan Tower. The ideal is the

maximum of speed in descending or ascending, not to be jolted into insensibility. There are two girl parts as beautifully thought out as the parts of ladies in love can be expected to be in Action Films. But in the end the love is not much more romantic in the eye of the spectator than it would be to behold a man on a motorcycle with the girl of his choice riding on the same machine behind him. And the highest type of Action Picture romance is not attained by having Juliet triumph over the motorcycle handicap. It is not achieved by weaving in a Sherlock Holmes plot. Action Picture romance comes when each hurdle is a tableau, when there is indeed an art-gallery-beauty in each one of these swift glimpses: when it is a race, but with a proper and golden-linked grace from action to action, and the goal is the most beautiful glimpse in the whole reel.

In the Action Picture there is no adequate means for the development of any full grown personal passion. The distinguished character-study that makes genuine the personal emotions in the legitimate drama, has no chance. People are but types, swiftly moved chessmen. More elaborate discourse on this subject may be found in chapter twelve on the differences between the

films and the stage. But here, briefly: the
Action Pictures are falsely advertised as having
heart-interest, or abounding in tragedy. But
though the actors glower and wrestle and even
if they are the most skilful lambasters in the
profession, the audience gossips and chews gum.

Why does the audience keep coming to this
type of photoplay if neither lust, love, hate,
nor hunger is adequately conveyed? Simply
because such spectacles gratify the incipient or
rampant speed-mania in every American.

To make the elevator go faster than the one
in the Metropolitan Tower is to destroy even
this emotion. To elaborate unduly any of the
agonies or seductions in the hope of arousing
lust, love, hate, or hunger, is to produce on
the screen a series of misplaced figures of the
order Frankenstein.

How often we have been horrified by these
galvanized and ogling corpses. These are the
things that cause the outcry for more censors.
It is not that our moral codes are insulted,
but what is far worse, our nervous systems are
temporarily racked to pieces. These wriggling
half-dead men, these over-bloody burglars, are
public nuisances, no worse and no better than
dead cats being hurled about by street urchins.

The cry for more censors is but the cry for the man with the broom. Sometimes it is a matter as simple as when a child is scratching with a pin on a slate. While one would not have the child locked up by the chief of police, after five minutes of it almost every one wants to smack him till his little jaws ache. It is the very cold-bloodedness of the proceeding that ruins our kindness of heart. And the best Action Film is impersonal and unsympathetic even if it has no scratching pins. Because it is cold-blooded it must take extra pains to be tactful. Cold-blooded means that the hero as we see him on the screen is a variety of amiable or violent ghost. Nothing makes his lack of human charm plainer than when we as audience enter the theatre at the middle of what purports to be the most passionate of scenes when the goal of the chase is unknown to us and the alleged "situation" appeals on its magnetic merits. Here is neither the psychic telepathy of Forbes Robertson's Cæsar, nor the fire-breath of E. H. Sothern's Don Quixote. The audience is not worked up into the deadly still mob-unity of the speaking theatre. We late comers wait for the whole reel to start over and the goal to be indicated in the preliminary, before we can get the least bit wrought up. The prize may be a lady's heart, the restoration of a lost reputation, or the ownership of the patent for a churn. In the more effective Action Plays it is often what would be secondary on the stage, the recovery of a certain glove, spade, bull-calf, or rock-quarry. And to begin, we are shown a clean-cut picture of said glove, spade, bull-calf, or rock-quarry. Then when these disappear from ownership or sight, the suspense continues till they are again visible on the screen in the hands of the rightful owner.

In brief, the actors hurry through what would be tremendous passions on the stage to recover something that can be really photographed. For instance, there came to our town long ago a film of a fight between Federals and Confederates, with the loss of many lives, all for the recapture of a steam-engine that took on more personality in the end than private or general on either side, alive or dead. It was based on the history of the very engine photographed, or else that engine was given in replica. The old locomotive was full of character and humor amidst the tragedy, leaking steam at every orifice. The original is in one of the Southern Civil War museums. This engine in its capacity as a principal actor is going to be referred to more than several times in this work.

The highest type of Action Picture gives us neither the quality of Macbeth or Henry Fifth, the Comedy of Errors, or the Taming of the Shrew. It gives us rather that fine and special quality that was in the ink-bottle of Robert Louis Stevenson, that brought about the limitations and the nobility of the stories of Kidnapped, Treasure Island, and the New Arabian Nights.

This discussion will be resumed on another plane in the eighth chapter: Sculpture-in-Motion.

Having read thus far, why not close the book and go round the corner to a photoplay theatre? Give the preference to the cheapest one. *The Action Picture will be inevitable. Since this chapter was written, Charlie Chaplin and Douglas Fairbanks have given complete department store examples of the method, especially Chaplin in the brilliantly constructed Shoulder Arms, and Fairbanks in his one great piece of acting, in The Three Musketeers.*

CHAPTER III

THE INTIMATE PHOTOPLAY

LET us take for our platform this sentence: THE MOTION PICTURE ART IS A GREAT HIGH ART, NOT A PROCESS OF COMMERCIAL MANUFACTURE. The people I hope to convince of this are (1) The great art museums of America, including the people who support them in any way, the people who give the current exhibitions there or attend them, the art school students in the corridors below coming on in the same field; (2) the departments of English, of the history of the drama, of the practice of the drama, and the history and practice of "art" in that amazingly long list of our colleges and universities — to be found, for instance, in the World Almanac; (3) the critical and literary world generally. Somewhere in this enormous field, piled with endowments mountain high, it should be possible to establish the theory and practice of the photoplay as a fine art. Readers who do

not care for the history of any art, readers
who have neither curiosity nor aspiration in
regard to any of the ten or eleven muses who
now dance around Apollo, such shabby readers
had best lay the book down now. Shabby
readers do not like great issues. My poor
little sermon is concerned with a great issue,
the clearing of the way for a critical standard,
whereby the ultimate photoplay may be judged.
I cannot teach office-boys ways to make
"quick money" in the "movies." That seems
to be the delicately implied purpose of the
mass of books on the photoplay subject. They
are, indeed, a sickening array. Freeburg's book
is one of the noble exceptions. And I have
paid tribute elsewhere to John Emerson and
Anita Loos. They have written a crusading
book, and many crusading articles.

After five years of exceedingly lonely art
study, in which I had always specialized in
museum exhibits, prowling around like a lost
dog, I began to intensify my museum study,
and at the same time shout about what I was
discovering. From nineteen hundred and five
on I did orate my opinions to a group of advanced students. We assembled weekly for
several winters in the Metropolitan Museum,

New York, for the discussion of the masterpieces in historic order, from Egypt to America.
From that standpoint, the work least often
found, hardest to make, least popular in the
street, may be in the end the one most treasured
in a world-museum as a counsellor and stimulus
of mankind. Throughout this book I try to
bring to bear the same simple standards of
form, composition, mood, and motive that we
used in finding the fundamental exhibits;
the standards which are taken for granted in
art histories and schools, radical or conserva-
tive, anywhere.

Again we assume it is eight o'clock in the
evening, friend reader, when the chapter
begins.

Just as the Action Picture has its photographic basis or fundamental metaphor in the
long chase down the highway, so the Intimate
Film has its photographic basis in the fact that
any photoplay interior has a very small ground
plan, and the cosiest of enclosing walls. Many
a worth-while scene is acted out in a space no
bigger than that which is occupied by an office
boy's stool and hat. If there is a table in this
room, it is often so near it is half out of the picture or perhaps it is against the front line of

the triangular ground-plan. Only the top of
the table is seen, and nothing close up to us is
pictured below that. We in the audience are
privileged characters. Generally attending the
show in bunches of two or three, we are members
of the household on the screen. Sometimes we
are sitting on the near side of the family board.
Or we are gossiping whispering neighbors, of
the shoemaker, we will say, with our noses
pressed against the pane of a metaphoric window.

Take for contrast the old-fashioned stage
production showing the room and work table
of a shoemaker. As it were the whole side
of the house has been removed. The shop
is as big as a banquet hall. There is something essentially false in what we see, no matter
how the stage manager fills in with old boxes,
broken chairs, and the like. But the photoplay interior is the size such a work-room should
be. And there the awl and pegs and bits of
leather, speaking the silent language of picture
writing, can be clearly shown. They are
sometimes like the engine in chapter two, the
principal actors.

Though the Intimate-and-friendly Photoplay
may be carried out of doors to the row of loafers

in front of the country store, or the gossiping streets of the village, it takes its origin and theory from the snugness of the interior.

The restless reader replies that he has seen photoplays that showed ball-rooms that were grandiose, not the least cosy. These are to be classed as out-of-door scenery so far as theory goes, and are to be discussed under the head of Splendor Pictures. Masses of human beings pour by like waves, the personalities of none made plain. The only definite people are the hero and heroine in the foreground, and maybe one other. Though these three be in ball-costume, the little triangle they occupy next to the camera is in sort an interior, while the impersonal guests behind them conform to the pageant principles of out-of-doors, and the dancers are to the main actor as is the wind-shaken forest to the charcoal-burner, or the bending grain to the reaper.

The Intimate Motion Picture is the world's new medium for studying, not the great passions, such as black hate, transcendent love, devouring ambition, but rather the half relaxed or gently restrained moods of human creatures. It gives also our idiosyncrasies. It is gossip *in extremis*. It is apt to chronicle our petty little skirmishes, rather than our feuds. In it Colin Clout and his comrades return.

The Intimate Photoplay should not crowd its characters. It should not choke itself trying to dramatize the whole big bloody plot of Lorna Doone, or any other novel with a dozen leading people. Yet some gentle episode from the John Ridd farm, some half-chapter when Lorna and the Doones are almost forgotten, would be fitting. Let the duck-yard be parading its best, and Annie among the milk-pails, her work for the evening well nigh done. The Vicar of Wakefield has his place in this form. The Intimate-and-friendly Motion Picture might very well give humorous moments in the lives of the great, King Alfred burning the cakes, and other legendary incidents of him. Plato's writings give us glimpses of Socrates, in between the long dialogues. And there are intimate scraps in Plutarch.

Prospective author-producer, do you remember Landor's Imaginary Conversations, and Lang's Letters to Dead Authors? Can you not attain to that informal understanding in pictorial delineations of such people?

The photoplay has been unjust to itself in comedies. The late John Bunny's important

place in my memory comes from the first picture in which I saw him. It is a story of
high life below stairs. The hero is the butler at
a governor's reception. John Bunny's work
as this man is a delightful piece of acting.
The servants are growing tipsier downstairs,
but the more afraid of the chief functionary
every time he appears, frozen into sobriety
by his glance. At the last moment this god of
the basement catches them at their worst and
gives them a condescending but forgiving
smile. The lid comes off completely. He
himself has been imbibing. His surviving
dignity in waiting on the governor's guests is
worthy of the stage of Goldsmith and Sheridan.
This film should be reissued in time as a Bunny
memorial.

So far as my experience has gone, the best
of the comedians is Sidney Drew. He could
shine in the atmosphere of Pride and Prejudice
or Cranford. But the best things I have seen
of his are far from such. I beg the pardon of
Miss Jane Austen and Mrs. Gaskell while I
mention Who's Who in Hogg's Hollow, and A
Regiment of Two. Over these I rejoiced like
a yokel with a pocketful of butterscotch and
peanuts. The opportunities to laugh on a

higher plane than this, to laugh like Olympians, are seldom given us in this world.

The most successful motion picture drama of the intimate type ever placed before mine eyes was Enoch Arden, produced by Cabanne.

Lillian Gish takes the part of Annie, Alfred Paget impersonates Enoch Arden, and Wallace Reid takes the part of Philip Ray. The play is in four reels of twenty minutes each. It should have been made into three reels by shortening every scene just a bit. Otherwise it is satisfying, and I and my friends have watched it through many times as it has returned to Springfield.

The mood of the original poem is approximated. The story is told with fireside friendliness. The pale Lillian Gish surrounded by happy children gives us many a genre painting on the theme of domesticity. It is a photographic rendering in many ways as fastidious as Tennyson's versification. The scenes on the desert island are some of them commonplace. The shipwreck and the like remind one of other photoplays, but the rest of the production has a mood of its own. Seen several months ago it fills my eye-imagination and eye-memory more than that particular piece of

Tennyson's fills word-imagination and word-memory.   Perhaps this is because it is pleasing to me as a theorist.   It is a sound example of the type of film to which this chapter is devoted.   If you cannot get your local manager to bring Enoch Arden, reread that poem of Tennyson's and translate it in your own mind's eye into a gallery of six hundred delicately toned photographs hung in logical order, most of them cosy interior scenes, some of the faces five feet from chin to forehead in the more personal episodes, yet exquisitely fair.   Fill in the out-of-door scenes and general gatherings with the appointments of an idyllic English fisher-village, and you will get an approximate conception of what we mean by the Intimate-and-friendly Motion Picture, or the Intimate Picture, as I generally call it, for convenience.

It is a quality, not a defect, of all photoplays that human beings tend to become dolls and mechanisms, and dolls and mechanisms tend to become human.   But the haughty, who scorn the moving pictures, cannot rid themselves of the feeling that they are being seduced into going into some sort of a Punch-and-Judy show.   And they think that of course one should not take seriously anything so cheap in price and so appealing to the cross-roads taste. But it is very well to begin in the Punch-and-Judy-show state of mind, and reconcile ourselves to it, and then like good democrats await discoveries. Punch and Judy is the simplest form of marionette performance, and the marionette has a place in every street in history just as the dolls' house has its corner in every palace and cottage. The French in particular have had their great periods of puppet shows; and the Italian tradition survived in America's Little Italy, in New York for many a day; and I will mention in passing that one of Pavlowa's unforgettable dance dramas is The Fairy Doll. Prospective author-producer, why not spend a deal of energy on the photoplay successors of the puppet-plays?

We have the queen of the marionettes already, without the play.

One description of the Intimate-and-friendly Comedy would be the Mary Pickford kind of a story. None has as yet appeared. But we know the Mary Pickford mood. When it is gentlest, most roguish, most exalted, it is a prophecy of what this type should be, not only in the actress, but in the scenario and setting.

Mary Pickford can be a doll, a village belle, or a church angel. Her powers as a doll are hinted at in the title of the production: Such a Little Queen. I remember her when she was a village belle in that film that came out before producers or actors were known by name. It was sugar-sweet. It was called: What the Daisy Said. If these productions had conformed to their titles sincerely, with the highest photoplay art we would have had two more examples for this chapter.

Why do the people love Mary? Not on account of the Daniel Frohman style of handling her appearances. He presents her to us in what are almost the old-fashioned stage terms: the productions energetic and full of painstaking detail but dominated by a dream that is a theatrical hybrid. It is neither good moving picture nor good stage play. Yet Mary could be cast as a cloudy Olympian or a church angel if her managers wanted her to be such. She herself was transfigured in the Dawn of Tomorrow, but the film-version of that play was merely a well mounted melodrama.

Why do the people love Mary? Because of a certain aspect of her face in her highest mood. Botticelli painted her portrait many centuries

ago when by some necromancy she appeared
to him in this phase of herself. There is in
the Chicago Art Institute at the top of the
stairs on the north wall a noble copy of a
fresco by that painter, the copy by Mrs. Mac-
Monnies. It is very near the Winged Victory
of Samothrace. In the picture the muses sit
enthroned. The loveliest of them all is a
startling replica of Mary.

The people are hungry for this fine and
spiritual thing that Botticelli painted in the
faces of his muses and heavenly creatures.
Because the mob catch the very glimpse of it
in Mary's face, they follow her night after
night in the films. They are never quite
satisfied with the plays, because the managers
are not artists enough to know they should
sometimes put her into sacred pictures and not
have her always the village hoyden, in plays
not even hoydenish. But perhaps in this argument I have but betrayed myself as Mary's in-
fatuated partisan.

So let there be recorded here the name of
another actress who is always in the intimate-
and-friendly mood and adapted to close-up
interiors, Marguerite Clark. She is endowed
by nature to act, in the same film, the eight-

year-old village pet, the irrepressible sixteen-
year-old, and finally the shining bride of twenty.
But no production in which she acts that has
happened to come under my eye has done
justice to these possibilities. The transitions
from one of these stages to the other are not
marked by the producer with sufficient delicate
graduation, emphasis, and contrast. Her plots
have been but sugared nonsense, or swash-
buckling ups and downs. She shines in a bevy
of girls. She has sometimes been given the
bevy.

But it is easier to find performers who fit
this chapter, than to find films. Having read so
far, it is probably not quite nine o'clock in the
evening. Go around the corner to the nearest
theatre. You will not be apt to find a pure
example of the Intimate-and-friendly Moving
Picture, but some one or two scenes will make
plain the intent of the phrase. Imagine the
most winsome tableau that passes before you,
extended logically through one or three reels,
with no melodramatic interruptions or awful
smashes. For a further discussion of these
smashes, and other items in this chapter,
read the ninth chapter, entitled "Painting-
in-Motion."

CHAPTER IV

THE MOTION PICTURE OF FAIRY SPLENDOR

AGAIN, kind reader, let us assume it is eight o'clock in the evening, for purposes of future climax which you no doubt anticipate.

Just as the Action Motion Picture has its photographic basis in the race down the highroad, just as the Intimate Motion Picture has its photographic basis in the close-up interior scene, so the Photoplay of Splendor, in its four forms, is based on the fact that the kinetoscope can take in the most varied of out-of-door landscapes. It can reproduce fairy dells. It can give every ripple of the lily-pond. It can show us cathedrals within and without. It can take in the panorama of cyclopæan cloud, bending forest, storm-hung mountain. In like manner it can put on the screen great impersonal mobs of men. It can give us tremendous armies, moving as oceans move. The pictures of Fairy Splendor, Crowd Splendor, Patriotic Splendor, and Religious Splendor are but the embodiments of these backgrounds.

And a photographic corollary quite useful in these four forms is that the camera has a kind of Hallowe'en witch-power. This power is the subject of this chapter.

The world-old legends and revelations of men in connection with the lovely out of doors, or lonely shrines, or derived from inspired crusading humanity moving in masses, can now be fitly retold. Also the fairy wand can do its work, the little dryad can come from the tree. And the spirits that guard the Republic can be seen walking on the clouds above the harvest-fields.

But we are concerned with the humblest voodooism at present.

Perhaps the world's oldest motion picture plot is a tale in Mother Goose. It ends somewhat in this fashion: —

> The old lady said to the cat: —
> "Cat, cat, kill rat.
> Rat will not gnaw rope,
> Rope will not hang butcher,
> Butcher will not kill ox,
> Ox will not drink water,
> Water will not quench fire,
> Fire will not burn stick,

Stick will not beat dog,
Dog will not bite pig,
Pig will not jump over the stile,
And I cannot get home to-night."

By some means the present writer does not remember, the cat was persuaded to approach the rat. The rest was like a tale of European diplomacy : —

The rat began to gnaw the rope,
The rope began to hang the butcher,
The butcher began to kill the ox,
The ox began to drink the water,
The water began to quench the fire,
The fire began to burn the stick,
The stick began to beat the dog,
The dog began to bite the pig,
The frightened little pig jumped over the stile,
And the old lady was able to get home that
    night.

Put yourself back to the state of mind in which you enjoyed this bit of verse.

Though the photoplay fairy-tale may rise to exquisite heights, it begins with pictures akin to this rhyme. Mankind in his childhood has always wanted his furniture to do such things. Arthur names his blade Excalibur. It becomes a person. The man in the Arabian tale speaks to the magic carpet. It carries him whithersoever he desires. This yearning for personality in furniture begins to be crudely worked upon in the so-called trick-scenes. The typical commercialized comedy of this sort is Moving Day. Lyman H. Howe, among many excellent reels of a different kind, has films allied to Moving Day.

But let us examine at this point, as even more typical, an old Pathé Film from France. The representatives of the moving-firm are sent for. They appear in the middle of the room with an astonishing jump. They are told that this household desires to have its goods and hearthstone gods transplanted two streets east. The agents salute. They disappear. Yet their wireless orders are obeyed with a military crispness. The books and newspapers climb out of the window. They go soberly down the street. In their wake are the dishes from the table. Then the more delicate porcelains climb down the shelves and follow. Then follow the hobble-de-hoy kitchen dishes, then the chairs, then the clothing, and the carpets from over the house. The most joyous and curious spectacle is to behold the shoes walking down the boulevard, from father's large boots to those of the youngest child. They form a complete satire of the family, yet have a masterful air of their own, as though they were the most important part of a human being.

The new apartment is shown. Everything enters in procession. In contrast to the general certainty of the rest, one or two pieces of furniture grow confused trying to find their places. A plate, in leaping upon a high shelf, misses and falls broken. The broom and dustpan sweep up the pieces, and consign them to the dustbin. Then the human family comes in, delighted to find everything in order. The moving agents appear and salute. They are paid their fee. They salute again and disappear with another gigantic leap.

The ability to do this kind of a thing is fundamental in the destinies of the art. Yet this resource is neglected because its special province is not understood. "People do not like to be tricked," the manager says. Certainly they become tired of mere contraptions. But they never grow weary of imagination. There is possible many a highly imaginative fairy-tale on this basis if we revert to the sound principles of the story of the old lady and the pig.

Moving Day is at present too crassly material. It has not the touch of the creative imagination. We are overwhelmed with a whole van of furniture. Now the mechanical or non-human object, beginning with the engine in the second chapter, is apt to be the hero in most any sort of photoplay while the producer remains utterly unconscious of the fact. Why not face this idiosyncrasy of the camera and make the non-human object the hero indeed? Not by filling the story with ropes, buckets, firebrands, and sticks, but by having these four unique. Make the fire the loveliest of torches, the water the most graceful of springs. Let the rope be the humorist. Let the stick be the outstanding hero, the D'Artagnan of the group, full of queer gestures and hoppings about. Let him be both polite and obdurate. Finally let him beat the dog most heroically.

Then, after the purely trick-picture is disciplined till it has fewer tricks, and those more human and yet more fanciful, the producer can move on up into the higher realms of the fairy-tale, carrying with him this riper workmanship.

Mabel Taliaferro's Cinderella, seen long ago,

is the best film fairy-tale the present writer
remembers. It has more of the fireside won-
der-spirit and Hallowe'en-witch-spirit than the
Cinderella of Mary Pickford.

There is a Japanese actor, Sessue Hayakawa,
who takes the leading part with Blanche
Sweet in The Clew, and is the hero in the film
version of The Typhoon. He looks like all
the actors in the old Japanese prints. He
has a general dramatic equipment which en-
ables him to force through the stubborn screen
such stagy plays as these, that are more
worth while in the speaking theatre. But
he has that atmosphere of pictorial romance
which would make him a valuable man for the
retelling of the old Japanese legends of Kwan-
non and other tales that are rich, unused moving picture material, tales such as have been
hinted at in the gleaming English of Lafcadio
Hearn.   The Japanese genius is eminently
pictorial. Rightly viewed, every Japanese
screen or bit of lacquer is from the Ancient
Asia Columbus set sail to find.

It would be a noble thing if American experts
in the Japanese principles of decoration, of the
school of Arthur W. Dow, should tell stories of
old Japan with the assistance of such men as

Sessue Hayakawa. Such things go further than peace treaties. Dooming a talent like that of Mr. Hayakawa to the task of interpreting the Japanese spy does not conduce to accord with Japan, however the technique may move us to admiration. Let such of us as are at peace get together, and tell the tales of our happy childhood to one another.

This chapter is ended. You will of course expect to be exhorted to visit some photoplay emporium. But you need not look for fairy-tales. They are much harder to find than they should be. But you can observe even in the advertisements and cartoons the technical elements of the story of the old lady and the pig. And you can note several other things that show how much more quickly than on the stage the borderline of All Saints' Day and Hallowe'en can be crossed. Note how easily memories are called up, and appear in the midst of the room. In any plays whatever, you will find these apparitions and recollections. The dullest hero is given glorious visualizing power. Note the "fadeaway" at the beginning and the end of the reel, whereby all things emerge from the twilight and sink back into the twilight at last. These are some of the indestructible least common denominators of folk stories old and new. When skilfully used, they can all exercise a power over the audience, such as the crystal has over the crystal-gazer.

But this discussion will be resumed, on another plane, in the tenth chapter: "Furniture, Trappings, and Inventions in Motion."

CHAPTER V

THE PICTURE OF CROWD SPLENDOR

HENCEFORTH the reader will use his discretion as to when he will read the chapter and when he will go to the picture show to verify it.

The shoddiest silent drama may contain noble views of the sea. This part is almost sure to be good. It is a fundamental resource.

A special development of this aptitude in the hands of an expert gives the sea of humanity, not metaphorically but literally: the whirling of dancers in ballrooms, handkerchief-waving masses of people in balconies, hat-waving political ratification meetings, ragged glowering strikers, and gossiping, dickering people in the market-place. Only Griffith and his close disciples can do these as well as almost any manager can reproduce the ocean. Yet the sea of humanity is dramatically blood-brother to the Pacific, Atlantic, or Mediterranean. It takes this new invention, the kinetoscope, to bring us these panoramic drama-elements. By the law of compensation, while the motion picture is shallow in showing private passion, it is powerful in conveying the passions of masses of men. Bernard Shaw, in a recent number of the Metropolitan, answered several questions in regard to the photoplay. Here are two bits from his discourse : —

"Strike the dialogue from Molière's Tartuffe, and what audience would bear its mere stage-business? Imagine the scene in which Iago poisons Othello's mind against Desdemona, conveyed in dumb show. What becomes of the difference between Shakespeare and Sheridan Knowles in the film? Or between Shakespeare's Lear and any one else's Lear? No, it seems to me that all the interest lies in the new opening for the mass of dramatic talent formerly disabled by incidental deficiencies of one sort or another that do not matter in the picture-theatre. . . ."

"Failures of the spoken drama may become the stars of the picture palace. And there are the authors with imagination, visualization and first-rate verbal gifts who can write novels and epics, but cannot for the life of them write plays. Well, the film lends itself admi-

rably to the succession of events proper to
narrative and epic, but physically impracticable
on the stage. Paradise Lost would make a
far better film than Ibsen's John Gabriel Borkman, though Borkman is a dramatic masterpiece, and Milton could not write an effective
play."

Note in especial what Shaw says about narrative, epic, and Paradise Lost.   He has in mind,
no doubt, the pouring hosts of demons and
angels.   This is one kind of a Crowd Picture.

There is another sort to be seen where George
Beban impersonates The Italian in a film of
that title, by Thomas H. Ince and G. Gardener
Sullivan.   The first part, taken ostensibly in
Venice, delineates the festival spirit of the people
on the bridges and in gondolas.   It gives out
the atmosphere of town-crowd happiness.
Then comes the vineyard, the crowd sentiment of a merry grape-harvest, then the
massed emotion of many people embarking
on an Atlantic liner telling good-by to
their kindred on the piers, then the drama
of arrival in New York.   The wonder of the
steerage people pouring down their proper
gangway is contrasted with the conventional
at-home-ness of the first-class passengers above.

Then we behold the seething human cauldron of the East Side, then the jolly little wedding-dance, then the life of the East Side, from the policeman to the peanut-man, and including the bar tender, for the crowd is treated on two separate occasions.

It is hot weather. The mobs of children follow the ice-wagon for chips of ice. They besiege the fountain-end of the street-sprinkling wagon quite closely, rejoicing to have their clothes soaked. They gather round the fire-plug that is turned on for their benefit, and again become wet as drowned rats.

Passing through these crowds are George Beban and Clara Williams as The Italian and his sweetheart. They owe the force of their acting to the fact that they express each mass of humanity in turn. Their child is born. It does not flourish. It represents in an acuter way another phase of the same child-struggle with the heat that the gamins indicate in their pursuit of the water-cart.

Then a deeper matter. The hero represents in a fashion the adventures of the whole Italian race coming to America : its natural southern gayety set in contrast to the drab East Side. The gondolier becomes boot-black.

The grape-gathering peasant girl becomes the suffering slum mother. They are not specialized characters like Pendennis or Becky Sharp in the Novels of Thackeray.

Omitting the last episode, the entrance into the house of Corrigan, The Italian is a strong piece of work.

Another kind of Crowd Picture is The Battle, an old Griffith Biograph, first issued in 1911, before Griffith's name or that of any actor in films was advertised. Blanche Sweet is the leading lady, and Charles H. West the leading man. The psychology of a bevy of village lovers is conveyed in a lively sweethearting dance. Then the boy and his comrades go forth to war. The lines pass between hand-waving crowds of friends from the entire neighborhood. These friends give the sense of patriotism in mass. Then as the consequence of this feeling, as the special agents to express it, the soldiers are in battle. By the fortunes of war the onset is unexpectedly near to the house where once was the dance.

The boy is at first a coward. He enters the old familiar door. He appeals to the girl to hide him, and for the time breaks her heart. He goes forth a fugitive not only from battle,

but from her terrible girlish anger. But later
he rallies. He brings a train of powder wagons
through fires built in his path by the enemy's
scouts. He loses every one of his men, and
all but the last wagon, which he drives himself. His return with that ammunition saves
the hard-fought day.

And through all this, glimpses of the battle
are given with a splendor that only Griffith
has attained.

Blanche Sweet stands as the representative
of the bevy of girls in the house of the dance,
and the whole body social of the village. How
the costumes flash and the handkerchiefs wave
around her! In the battle the hero represents
the cowardice that all the men are resisting
within themselves. When he returns, he is
the incarnation of the hardihood they have
all hoped to display. Only the girl knows he
was first a failure. The wounded general
honors him as the hero above all. Now she
is radiant, she cannot help but be triumphant,
though the side of the house is blown out by a
shell and the dying are everywhere.

This one-reel work of art has been reissued
of late by the Biograph Company. It should
be kept in the libraries of the Universities as a

standard. One-reel films are unfortunate in this
sense that in order to see a favorite the student
must wait through five other reels of a mixed programme that usually is bad. That is the reason
one-reel masterpieces seldom appear now. The
producer in a mood to make a special effort wants
to feel that he has the entire evening, and that
nothing before or after is going to be a bore or
destroy the impression. So at present the painstaking films are apt to be five or six reels of
twenty minutes each. These have the advantage that if they please at all, one can see
them again at once without sitting through
irrelevant slap-stick work put there to fill out
the time. But now, having the whole evening
to work in, the producer takes too much time
for his good ideas. I shall reiterate throughout this work the necessity for restraint.
A one hour programme is long enough for
any one. If the observer is pleased, he will
sit it through again and take another hour.
There is not a good film in the world but is
the better for being seen in immediate succession to itself. Six-reel programmes are a
weariness to the flesh. The best of the old
one-reel Biographs of Griffith contained more
in twenty minutes than these ambitious incon-

tinent six-reel displays give us in two hours. It would pay a manager to hang out a sign: "This show is only twenty minutes long, but it is Griffith's great film 'The Battle.'"

But I am digressing. To continue the contrast between private passion in the theatre and crowd-passion in the photoplay, let us turn to Shaw again. Consider his illustration of Iago, Othello, and Lear. These parts, as he implies, would fall flat in motion pictures. The minor situations of dramatic intensity might in many cases be built up. The crisis would inevitably fail. Iago and Othello and Lear, whatever their offices in their governments, are essentially private persons, individuals *in extremis*. If you go to a motion picture and feel yourself suddenly gripped by the highest dramatic tension, as on the old stage, and reflect afterward that it was a fight between only two or three men in a room otherwise empty, stop to analyze what they stood for. They were probably representatives of groups or races that had been pursuing each other earlier in the film. Otherwise the conflict, however violent, appealed mainly to the sense of speed.

So, in The Birth of a Nation, which could better be called The Overthrow of Negro

Rule, the Ku Klux Klan dashes down the road as powerfully as Niagara pours over the cliff. Finally the white girl Elsie Stoneman (impersonated by Lillian Gish) is rescued by the Ku Klux Klan from the mulatto politician, Silas Lynch (impersonated by George Seigmann). The lady is brought forward as a typical helpless white maiden. The white leader, Col. Ben Cameron (impersonated by Henry B. Walthall), enters not as an individual, but as representing the whole Anglo-Saxon Niagara. He has the mask of the Ku Klux Klan on his face till the crisis has passed. The wrath of the Southerner against the blacks and their Northern organizers has been piled up through many previous scenes. As a result this rescue is a real climax, something the photoplays that trace strictly personal hatreds cannot achieve.

The Birth of a Nation is a Crowd Picture in a triple sense. On the films, as in the audience, it turns the crowd into a mob that is either for or against the Reverend Thomas Dixon's poisonous hatred of the negro.

Griffith is a chameleon in interpreting his authors. Wherever the scenario shows traces of The Clansman, the original book, by Thomas Dixon, it is bad. Wherever it is unadulterated

Griffith, which is half the time, it is good. The Reverend Thomas Dixon is a rather stagy Simon Legree: in his avowed views a deal like the gentleman with the spiritual hydrophobia in the latter end of Uncle Tom's Cabin. Unconsciously Mr. Dixon has done his best to prove that Legree was not a fictitious character.

Joel Chandler Harris, Harry Stillwell Edwards, George W. Cable, Thomas Nelson Page, James Lane Allen, and Mark Twain are Southern men in Mr. Griffith's class. I recommend their works to him as a better basis for future Southern scenarios.

The Birth of a Nation has been very properly denounced for its Simon Legree qualities by Francis Hackett, Jane Addams, and others. But it is still true that it is a wonder in its Griffith sections. In its handling of masses of men it further illustrates the principles that made notable the old one-reel Battle film described in the beginning of this chapter. The Battle in the end is greater, because of its self-possession and concentration: all packed into twenty minutes.

When, in The Birth of a Nation, Lincoln (impersonated by Joseph Henabery) goes down

before the assassin, it is a master-scene. He
falls as the representative of the government and
a thousand high and noble crowd aspirations.
The mimic audience in the restored Ford's
Theatre rises in panic. This crowd is interpreted in especial for us by the two young
people in the seats nearest, and the freezing
horror of the treason sweeps from the Ford's
Theatre audience to the real audience beyond
them. The real crowd touched with terror
beholds its natural face in the glass.

Later come the pictures of the rioting negroes
in the streets of the Southern town, mobs
splendidly handled, tossing wildly and rhythmi-
cally like the sea. Then is delineated the rise of
the Ku Klux Klan, of which we have already
spoken. For comment on the musical accompaniment to The Birth of a Nation, read the
fourteenth chapter entitled "The Orchestra,
Conversation and the Censorship."

In the future development of motion pictures mob-movements of anger and joy will
go through fanatical and provincial whirlwinds
into great national movements of anger and joy.

A book by Gerald Stanley Lee that has a
score of future scenarios in it, a book that might
well be dipped into by the reader before he

goes to such a play as The Italian or The Battle, is the work which bears the title of this chapter: " Crowds."

Mr. Lee is far from infallible in his remedies for factory and industrial relations. But in sensitiveness to the flowing street of humanity he is indeed a man. Listen to the names of some of the divisions of his book: "Crowds and Machines; Letting the Crowds be Good; Letting the Crowds be Beautiful; Crowds and Heroes; Where are we Going? The Crowd Scare; The Strike, an Invention for making Crowds Think; The Crowd's Imagination about People; Speaking as One of the Crowd; Touching the Imagination of Crowds." Films in the spirit of these titles would help to make world-voters of us all.

The World State is indeed far away. But as we peer into the Mirror Screen some of us dare to look forward to the time when the pouring streets of men will become sacred in each other's eyes, in pictures and in fact.

A further discussion of this theme on other planes will be found in the eleventh chapter, entitled "Architecture-in-Motion," and the fifteenth chapter, entitled " The Substitute for the Saloon."

CHAPTER VI

THE Patriotic Picture need not necessarily be in terms of splendor. It generally is. Beginning the chronicle is one that waves no banners.

The Typhoon, a film produced by Thomas H. Ince, is a story of the Japanese love of Nippon in which a very little of the landscape of the nation is shown, and that in the beginning. The hero (acted by Sessue Hayakawa), living in the heart of Paris, represents the far-off Empire. He is making a secret military report. He is a responsible member of a colony of Japanese gentlemen. The bevy of them appear before or after his every important action. He still represents this crowd when alone.

The unfortunate Parisian heroine, unable to fathom the mystery of the fanatical hearts of the colony, ventures to think that her love for the Japanese hero and his equally great devotion to her is the important human relation on the horizon. She flouts his obscure work, pits her charms against it. In the end there is a quarrel. The irresistible meets the immovable, and in madness or half by accident, he kills the girl.

The youth is protected by the colony, for he alone can make the report. He is the machine-like representative of the Japanese patriotic formula, till the document is complete. A new arrival in the colony, who obviously cannot write the book, confesses the murder and is executed. The other high fanatic dies soon after, of a broken heart, with the completed manuscript volume in his hand. The one impression of the play is that Japanese patriotism is a peculiar and fearful thing. The particular quality of the private romance is but vaguely given, for such things in their rise and culmination can only be traced by the novelist, or by the gentle alternations of silence and speech on the speaking stage, aided by the hot blood of players actually before us.

Here, as in most photoplays, the attempted lover-conversations in pantomime are but indifferent things. The details of the hero's last quarrel with the heroine and the precise

thoughts that went with it are muffled by the
inability to speak. The power of the play is
in the adequate style the man represents the colony. Sessue Hayakawa should give us Japanese tales more adapted to the films. We
should have stories of Iyeyasu and Hideyoshi,
written from the ground up for the photoplay
theatre. We should have the story of the
Forty-seven Ronin, not a Japanese stage version, but a work from the source-material.
We should have legends of the various clans,
picturizations of the code of the Samurai.

The Typhoon is largely indoors. But the
Patriotic Motion Picture is generally a landscape. This is for deeper reasons than that
it requires large fields in which to manœuvre
armies. Flags are shown for other causes
than that they are the nominal signs of a love
of the native land.

In a comedy of the history of a newspaper,
the very columns of the publication are
actors, and may be photographed oftener than
the human hero. And in the higher realms
this same tendency gives particular power to
the panorama and trappings. It makes the
natural and artificial magnificence more than
a narrative, more than a color-scheme, some-

thing other than a drama. In a photoplay
by a master, when the American flag is shown,
the thirteen stripes are columns of history
and the stars are headlines. The woods and
the templed hills are their printing press, almost in a literal sense.

Going back to the illustration of the engine,
in chapter two, the non-human thing is a personality, even if it is not beautiful. When it
takes on the ritual of decorative design, this
new vitality is made seductive, and when it is
an object of nature, this seductive ritual becomes a new pantheism. The armies upon
the mountains they are defending are rooted
in the soil like trees. They resist invasion
with the same elementary stubbornness with
which the oak resists the storm or the cliff
resists the wave.

Let the reader consider Antony and Cleopatra, the Cines film. It was brought to
America from Italy by George Klein. This
and several ambitious spectacles like it are
direct violations of the foregoing principles.
True, it glorifies Rome. It is equivalent to
waving the Italian above the Egyptian flag,
quite slowly for two hours. From the stage

standpoint, the magnificence is thoroughgoing.
Viewed as a circus, the acting is elephantine
in its grandeur. All that is needed is pink
lemonade sold in the audience.

The famous Cabiria, a tale of war between
Rome and Carthage, by D'Annunzio, is a
prime example of a success, where Antony
and Cleopatra and many European films
founded upon the classics have been failures. With obvious defects as a producer,
D'Annunzio appreciates spectacular symbolism.
He has an instinct for the strange and the
beautifully infernal, as they are related to
decorative design. Therefore he is able to
show us Carthage indeed. He has an Italian
patriotism that amounts to frenzy. So Rome
emerges body and soul from the past, in this
spectacle. He gives us the cruelty of Baal,
the intrepidity of the Roman legions. Everything Punic or Italian in the middle distance
or massed background speaks of the very
genius of the people concerned and actively
generates their kind of lightning.

The principals do not carry out the momentum of this immense resource. The half a
score of leading characters, with the costumes,
gestures, and aspects of gods, are after all

works of the taxidermist. They are stuffed
gods. They conduct a silly nickelodeon romance while Carthage rolls on toward her doom.
They are like sparrows fighting for grain on
the edge of the battle.

The doings of his principals are sufficiently
evident to be grasped with a word or two of
printed insert on the films. But he senti-
mentalizes about them. He adds side-elabo-
rations of the plot that would require much
time to make clear, and a hard working novelist to make interesting. We are sentenced to
stop and gaze long upon this array of printing
in the darkness, just at the moment the tenth
wave of glory seems ready to sweep in. But
one hundred words cannot be a photoplay
climax. The climax must be in a tableau
that is to the eye as the rising sun itself, that
follows the thousand flags of the dawn.

In the New York performance, and pre-
sumably in other large cities, there was also
an orchestra. Behold then, one layer of great
photoplay, one layer of bad melodrama, one
layer of explanation, and a final cement of
music. It is as though in an art museum there
should be a man at the door selling would-be
masterly short-stories about the paintings,

and a man with a violin playing the catalogue. But for further discourse on the orchestra read the fourteenth chapter.

I left Cabiria with mixed emotions. And I had to forget the distressful eye-strain. Few eyes submit without destruction to three hours of film. But the mistakes of Cabiria are those of the pioneer work of genius. It has in it twenty great productions. It abounds in suggestions. Once the classic rules of this art-unit are established, men with equal genius with D'Annunzio and no more devotion, will give us the world's masterpieces. As it is, the background and mass-movements must stand as monumental achievements in vital patriotic splendor.

D'Annunzio is Griffith's most inspired rival in these things. He lacks Griffith's knowledge of what is photoplay and what is not. He lacks Griffith's simplicity of hurdle-race plot. He lacks his avalanche-like action. The Italian needs the American's health and clean winds. He needs his foregrounds, leading actors, and types of plot. But the American has never gone as deep as the Italian into landscapes that are their own tragedians, and into Satanic and celestial ceremonials.

Judith of Bethulia and The Battle Hymn of the Republic have impressed me as the two most significant photoplays I have ever encountered. They may be classed with equal justice as religious or patriotic productions. But for reasons which will appear, The Battle Hymn of the Republic will be classed as a film of devotion and Judith as a patriotic one. The latter was produced by D. W. Griffith, and released by the Biograph Company in 1914. The original stage drama was once played by the famous Boston actress, Nance O'Neil. It is the work of Thomas Bailey Aldrich. The motion picture scenario, when Griffith had done with it, had no especial Aldrich flavor, though it contained several of the characters and events as Aldrich conceived them. It was principally the old apocryphal story plus the genius of Griffith and that inner circle of players whom he has endowed with much of his point of view.

This is his cast of characters: —

Judith	Blanche Sweet
Holofernes	Henry Walthall
His servant	J. J. Lance
Captain of the } Guards } . .	H. Hyde

Judith's maid   .   .   .   Miss Bruce

General of the ⎫
   Jews   ⎭ .   .   .   C. H. Mailes

Priests · · · · · · ⎰ Messrs. Oppleman and
                        ⎱   Lestina

Nathan . . . . . Robert Harron

Naomi . . . . . . Mae Marsh

Keeper of the slaves ⎫
   for Holofernes   ⎭ · Alfred Paget

The Jewish ⎫
   mother ⎭ . . . Lillian Gish

The Biograph Company advertises the production with the following Barnum and Bailey enumeration: "In four parts. Produced in California. Most expensive Biograph ever produced. More than one thousand people and about three hundred horsemen. The following were built expressly for the production: a replica of the ancient city of Bethulia; the mammoth wall that protected Bethulia; a faithful reproduction of the ancient army camps, embodying all their barbaric splendor and dances; chariots, battering rams, scaling ladders, archer towers, and other special war paraphernalia of the period.

"The following spectacular effects: the storm-

ing of the walls of the city of Bethulia;
the hand-to-hand conflicts; the death-defying
chariot charges at break-neck speed; the rear-
ing and plunging horses infuriated by the din of
battle; the wonderful camp of the terrible
Holofernes, equipped with rugs brought from
the far East; the dancing girls in their exhibition of the exquisite and peculiar dances of
the period; the routing of the command of the
terrible Holofernes, and the destruction of
the camp by fire. And overshadowing all,
the heroism of the beautiful Judith."

This advertisement should be compared
with the notice of Your Girl and Mine tran-
scribed in the seventeenth chapter.

But there is another point of view by which
this Judith of Bethulia production may be
approached, however striking the advertising
notice.

There are four sorts of scenes alternated:
(1) the particular history of Judith; (2) the
gentle courtship of Nathan and Naomi, types
of the inhabitants of Bethulia; (3) pictures
of the streets, with the population flowing
like a sluggish river; (4) scenes of raid, camp,
and battle, interpolated between these, tying
the whole together. The real plot is the bal-

anced alternation of all the elements. So many minutes of one, then so many minutes of another. As was proper, very little of the tale was thrown on the screen in reading matter, and no climax was ever a printed word, but always an enthralling tableau.

The particular history of Judith begins with the picture of her as the devout widow. She is austerely garbed, at prayer for her city, in her own quiet house. Then later she is shown decked for the eyes of man in the camp of Holofernes, where all is Assyrian glory. Judith struggles between her unexpected love for the dynamic general and the resolve to destroy him that brought her there. In either type of scene, the first gray and silver, the other painted with Paul Veronese splendor, Judith moves with a delicate deliberation. Over her face the emotions play like winds on a meadow lake. Holofernes is the composite picture of all the Biblical heathen chieftains. His every action breathes power. He is an Assyrian bull, a winged lion, and a god at the same time, and divine honors are paid to him every moment.

Nathan and Naomi are two Arcadian lovers. In their shy meetings they express the life of the normal Bethulia. They are seen among the reapers outside the city or at the well near the wall, or on the streets of the ancient town. They are generally doing the things the crowd behind them is doing, meanwhile evolving their own little heart affair. Finally when the Assyrian comes down like a wolf on the fold, the gentle Naomi becomes a prisoner in Holofernes' camp. She is in the foreground, a representative of the crowd of prisoners. Nathan is photographed on the wall as the particular defender of the town in whom we are most interested.

The pictures of the crowd's normal activities avoid jerkiness and haste. They do not abound in the boresome self-conscious quietude that some producers have substituted for the usual twitching. Each actor in the assemblies has a refreshing equipment in gentle gesticulation; for the manners and customs of Bethulia must needs be different from those of America. Though the population moves together as a river, each citizen is quite preoccupied. To the furthest corner of the picture, they are egotistical as human beings. The elder goes by, in theological conversation with his friend. He thinks his theology is important. The mother goes by, all absorbed in her child. To her it is the only child in the world.

Alternated with these scenes is the terrible rush of the Assyrian army, on to exploration, battle, and glory. The speed of their setting out becomes actual, because it is contrasted with the deliberation of the Jewish town. At length the Assyrians are along those hills and valleys and below the wall of defence. The population is on top of the battlements, beating them back the more desperately because they are separated from the water-supply, the wells in the fields where once the lovers met. In a lull in the siege, by a connivance of the elders, Judith is let out of a little door in the wall. And while the fortune of her people is most desperate she is shown in the quiet shelter of the tent of Holofernes. Sinuous in grace, tranced, passionately in love, she has forgotten her peculiar task. She is in a sense Bethulia itself, the race of Israel made over into a woman, while Holofernes is the embodiment of the besieging army. Though in a quiet tent, and on the terms of love, it is the essential warfare of the hot Assyrian blood and the pure and peculiar Jewish thoroughbredness.

Blanche Sweet as Judith is indeed dignified
and ensnaring, the more so because in her
abandoned quarter of an hour the Jewish
sanctity does not leave her. And her aged
woman attendant, coming in and out, sentinel
and conscience, with austere face and lifted
finger, symbolizes the fire of Israel that shall
yet awaken within her. When her love for
her city and God finally becomes paramount,
she shakes off the spell of the divine honors
which she has followed all the camp in according to that living heathen deity Holofernes,
and by the very transfiguration of her figure
and countenance we know that the deliverance
of Israel is at hand. She beheads the dark
Assyrian. Soon she is back in the city, by
way of the little gate by which she emerged.
The elders receive her and her bloody trophy.

The people who have been dying of thirst
arise in a final whirlwind of courage. Bereft
of their military genius, the Assyrians flee
from the burning camp. Naomi is delivered
by her lover Nathan. This act is taken by
the audience as a type of the setting free of all
the captives. Then we have the final return
of the citizens to their town. As for Judith,
hers is no crass triumph. She is shown in her

gray and silvery room in her former widow's
dress, but not the same woman. There is
thwarted love in her face. The sword of
sorrow is there. But there is also the prayer
of thanksgiving. She goes forth. She is hailed
as her city's deliverer. She stands among the
nobles like a holy candle.

Providing the picture may be preserved in its
original delicacy, it has every chance to retain
a place in the affections of the wise, if a humble pioneer of criticism may speak his honest
mind.

Though in this story the archaic flavor is
well-preserved, the way the producer has pictured the population at peace, in battle, in
despair, in victory gives me hope that he or
men like unto him will illustrate the American patriotic crowd-prophecies. We must
have Whitmanesque scenarios, based on moods
akin to that of the poem By Blue Ontario's
Shore. The possibility of showing the entire
American population its own face in the Mirror
Screen has at last come. Whitman brought
the idea of democracy to our sophisticated
literati, but did not persuade the democracy
itself to read his democratic poems. Sooner
or later the kinetoscope will do what he could

not, bring the nobler side of the equality idea to the people who are so crassly equal.

The photoplay penetrates in our land to the haunts of the wildest or the dullest. The isolated prospector rides twenty miles to see the same film that is displayed on Broadway. There is not a civilized or half-civilized land but may read the Whitmanesque message in time, if once it is put on the films with power. Photoplay theatres are set up in ports where sailors revel, in heathen towns where gentlemen adventurers are willing to make one last throw with fate.

On the other hand, as a recorder Whitman approaches the wildest, rawest American material and conquers it, at the same time keeping his nerves in the state in which Swinburne wrote Only the Song of Secret Bird, or Lanier composed The Ballad of Trees and The Master. J. W. Alexander's portrait of Whitman in the Metropolitan Museum, New York, is not too sophisticated. The out-of-door profoundness of this poet is far richer than one will realize unless he has just returned from some cross-country adventure afoot. Then if one reads breathlessly by the page and the score of pages, there is a glory

transcendent. For films of American patriotism to parallel the splendors of Cabiria
and Judith of Bethulia, and to excel them, let
us have Whitmanesque scenarios based on
moods like that of By Blue Ontario's Shore,
The Salute au Monde, and The Passage to
India. Then the people's message will reach
the people at last.

The average Crowd Picture will cling close
to the streets that are, and the usual Patriotic
Picture will but remind us of nationality as it
is at present conceived and aflame, and the
Religious Picture will for the most part
be close to the standard orthodoxies. The
final forms of these merge into each other,
though they approach the heights by different
avenues. We Americans should look for the
great photoplay of tomorrow, that will mark
a decade or a century, that prophesies of the
flags made one, the crowds in brotherhood.

CHAPTER VII

RELIGIOUS SPLENDOR

As far as the photoplay is concerned, religious emotion is a form of crowd-emotion. In the most conventional and rigid church sense this phase can be conveyed more adequately by the motion picture than by the stage. There is little, of course, for the anti-ritualist in the art-world anywhere. The thing that makes cathedrals real shrines in the eye of the reverent traveller makes them, with their religious processions and the like, impressive in splendor-films.

For instance, I have long remembered the essentials of the film, The Death of Thomas Becket. It may not compare in technique with some of our present moving picture achievements, but the idea must have been particularly adapted to the film medium. The story has stayed in my mind with great persistence, not only as a narrative, but as the first hint to me that orthodox religious feeling has here an undeveloped field.

Green tells the story in this way, in his History of the English People : —

"Four knights of the King's court, stirred to outrage by a passionate outburst of their master's wrath, crossed the sea and on the twenty-ninth of December forced their way into the Archbishop's palace. After a stormy parley with him in his chamber they withdrew to arm. Thomas was hurried by his clerks into the cathedral, but as he reached the steps leading from the transept into the choir his pursuers burst in from the cloisters. 'Where,' cried Reginald Fitzurse, 'is the traitor, Thomas Becket?' 'Here am I, no traitor, but a priest of God,' he replied. And again descending the steps he placed himself with his back against a pillar and fronted his foes. . . . The brutal murder was received with a thrill of horror throughout Christendom. Miracles were wrought at the martyr's tomb, etc. . . ."

It is one of the few deaths in moving pictures that have given me the sense that I was watching a tragedy. Most of them affect one, if they have any effect, like exhibits in an art gallery, as does Josef Israels' oil painting, Alone in the World. We admire the tech-

nique, and as for emotion, we feel the pictur-
esqueness only. But here the church procession,
the robes, the candles, the vaulting overhead,
the whole visualized cathedral mood has the
power over the reverent eye it has in life, and
a touch more.

It is not a private citizen who is struck down.
Such a taking off would have been but nominally impressive, no matter how well acted.
Private deaths in the films, to put it another
way, are but narrative statements. It is not
easy to convey their spiritual significance.
Take, for instance, the death of John Goderic,
in the film version of Gilbert Parker's The
Seats of the Mighty. The major leaves this
world in the first third of the story. The photoplay use of his death is, that he may whisper in
the ear of Robert Moray to keep certain letters
of La Pompadour well hidden. The fact that
it is the desire of a dying man gives sharpness to his request. Later in the story Moray
is hard-pressed by the villain for those same
papers. Then the scene of the death is flashed
for an instant on the screen, representing the
hero's memory of the event. It is as though
he should recollect and renew a solemn oath.
The documents are more important than John

Goderic. His departure is but one of their attributes. So it is in any film. There is no emotional stimulation in the final departure of a non-public character to bring tears, such tears as have been provoked by the novel or the stage over the death of Sidney Carton or Faust's Marguerite or the like.

All this, to make sharper the fact that the murder of Becket the archbishop is a climax. The great Church and hierarchy are profaned. The audience feels the same thrill of horror that went through Christendom. We understand why miracles were wrought at the martyr's tomb.

In the motion pictures the entrance of a child into the world is a mere family episode, not a climax, when it is the history of private people. For instance, several little strangers come into the story of Enoch Arden. They add beauty, and are links in the chain of events. Still they are only one of many elements of idyllic charm in the village of Annie. Something that in real life is less valuable than a child is the goal of each tiny tableau, some coming or departure or the like that affects the total plot. But let us imagine a production that would chronicle the promise to Abraham, and the vision that came with it. Let the film

show the final gift of Isaac to the aged Sarah,
even the boy who is the beginning of a race that
shall be as the stars of heaven and the sands
of the sea for multitude. This could be made
a pageant of power and glory. The crowd-
emotions, patriotic fires, and religious exalta-
tions on which it turns could be given in noble
procession and the tiny fellow on the pillow
made the mystic centre of the whole. The
story of the coming of Samuel, the dedicated
little prophet, might be told on similar terms.

The real death in the photoplay is the ritualistic death, the real birth is the ritualistic
birth, and the cathedral mood of the motion
picture which goes with these and is close to
these in many of its phases, is an inexhaustible
resource.

The film corporations fear religious questions,
lest offence be given to this sect or that. So
let such denominations as are in the habit of
coöperating, themselves take over this medium,
not gingerly, but whole-heartedly, as in mediæval time the hierarchy strengthened its hold
on the people with the marvels of Romanesque
and Gothic architecture. This matter is further discussed in the seventeenth chapter, entitled "Progress and Endowment."

But there is a field wherein the commercial man will not be accused of heresy or sacrilege, which builds on ritualistic birth and death and elements akin thereto. This the established producer may enter without fear. Which brings us to The Battle Hymn of the Republic, issued by the American Vitagraph Company in 1911. This film should be studied in the High Schools and Universities till the canons of art for which it stands are established in America. The director was Larry Trimble. All honor to him.

The patriotism of The Battle Hymn of the Republic, if taken literally, deals with certain aspects of the Civil War. But the picture is transfigured by so marked a devotion, that it is the main illustration in this work of the religious photoplay.

The beginning shows President Lincoln in the White House brooding over the lack of response to his last call for troops. (He is impersonated by Ralph Ince.) He and Julia Ward Howe are looking out of the window on a recruiting headquarters that is not busy. (Mrs. Howe is impersonated by Julia S. Gordon.) Another scene shows an old mother in the West refusing to let her son enlist. (This woman

is impersonated by Mrs. Maurice.)   The father
has died in the war.   The sword hangs on the
wall.   Later Julia Ward Howe is shown in her
room asleep at midnight, then rising in a trance
and writing the Battle Hymn at a table by the
bed.

The pictures that might possibly have passed
before her mind during the trance are thrown
upon the screen.   The phrases they illustrate
are not in the final order of the poem, but in
the possible sequence in which they went on
the paper in the first sketch.   The dream
panorama is not a literal discussion of aboli-
tionism or states' rights.   It illustrates rather
the Hebraic exultation applied to all lands and
times.   "Mine eyes have seen the glory of the
coming of the Lord"; a gracious picture of the
nativity.   (Edith Storey impersonates Mary the
Virgin.)   "I have seen him in the watchfires
of a hundred circling camps" and "They have
builded him an altar in the evening dews and
damps" — for these are given symbolic pageants
of the Holy Sepulchre crusaders.

Then there is a visible parable, showing a
marketplace in some wicked capital, neither
Babylon, Tyre, nor Nineveh, but all of them
in essential character.   First come spectacles

of rejoicing, cruelty, and waste. Then from
Heaven descend flood and fire, brimstone and
lightning. It is like the judgment of the
Cities of the Plain. Just before the overthrow,
the line is projected upon the screen : "He hath
loosed the fateful lightning of his terrible swift
sword." Then the heavenly host becomes gradually visible upon the air, marching toward the
audience, almost crossing the footlights, and
blowing their solemn trumpets. With this
picture the line is given us to read : "Our God
is marching on." This host appears in the
photoplay as often as the refrain sweeps into
the poem. The celestial company, its imper-
ceptible emergence, its spiritual power when in
the ascendant, is a thing never to be forgotten,
a tableau that proves the motion picture a
great religious instrument.

Then comes a procession indeed. It is as
though the audience were standing at the side
of the throne at Doomsday looking down the
hill of Zion toward the little earth. There is a
line of those who are to be judged, leaders
from the beginning of history, barbarians with
their crude weapons, classic characters, Cæsar
and his rivals for fame; mediæval figures including Dante meditating; later figures, Riche-

lieu, Napoleon. Many people march toward the strange glorifying eye of the camera, growing larger than men, filling the entire field of vision, disappearing when they are almost upon us. The audience weighs the worth of their work to the world as the men themselves with downcast eyes seem to be doing also. The most thrilling figure is Tolstoi in his peasant smock, coming after the bitter egotists and conquerors. (The impersonation is by Edward Thomas.) I shall never forget that presence marching up to the throne invisible with bowed head. This procession is to illustrate the line: "He is sifting out the hearts of men before his Judgment Seat." Later Lincoln is pictured on the steps of the White House. It is a quaint tableau, in the spirit of the old-fashioned Rogers group. Yet it is masterful for all that. Lincoln is taking the chains from a cowering slave. This tableau is to illustrate the line: "Let the hero born of woman crush the serpent with his heel." Now it is the end of the series of visions. It is morning in Mrs. Howe's room. She rises. She is filled with wonder to find the poem on her table.

Written to the rousing glory-tune of John Brown's Body the song goes over the North

like wildfire. The far-off home of the widow
is shown. She and the boy read the famous
chant in the morning news column. She takes
the old sword from the wall. She gives it to
her son and sends him to enlist with her blessing. In the next picture Lincoln and Mrs. Howe
are looking out of the window where was once
the idle recruiting tent. A new army is pouring by, singing the words that have rallied the
nation. Ritualistic birth and death have been
discussed. This film might be said to illustrate
ritualistic birth, death, and resurrection.

The writer has seen hundreds of productions
since this one. He has described it from
memory. It came out in a time when the
American people paid no attention to the producer or the cast. It may have many technical
crudities by present-day standards. But the
root of the matter is there. And Springfield
knew it. It was brought back to our town
many times. It was popular in both the fash-
ionable picture show houses and the cheapest,
dirtiest hole in the town. It will soon be reissued by the Vitagraph Company. Every
student of American Art should see this film.

The same exultation that went into it, the
faculty for commanding the great spirits of

history and making visible the unseen powers of the air, should be applied to Crowd Pictures which interpret the non-sectarian prayers of the broad human race.

The pageant of Religious Splendor is the final photoplay form in the classification which this work seeks to establish. Much of what follows will be to reënforce the heads of these first discourses. Further comment on the Religious Photoplay may be found in the eleventh chapter, entitled "Architecture-in-Motion."

CHAPTER VIII

THE outline is complete. Now to reënforce it. Pictures of Action Intimacy and Splendor are the foundation colors in the photoplay, as red, blue, and yellow are the basis of the rainbow. Action Films might be called the red section; Intimate Motion Pictures, being colder and quieter, might be called blue; and Splendor Photoplays called yellow, since that is the hue of pageants and sunshine.

Another way of showing the distinction is to review the types of gesture. The Action Photoplay deals with generalized pantomime: the gesture of the conventional policeman in contrast with the mannerism of the stereo-typed preacher. The Intimate Film gives us more elusive personal gestures: the difference between the table manners of two preachers in the same restaurant, or two policemen. A mark of the Fairy Play is the gesture of incantation, the sweep of the arm whereby Mab would transform a prince into a hawk. The other Splendor Films deal with the total gestures of crowds: the pantomime of a torch-waving mass of men, the drill of an army on the march, or the bending of the heads of a congregation receiving the benediction.

Another way to demonstrate the thesis is to use the old classification of poetry: dramatic, lyric, epic. The Action Play is a narrow form of the dramatic. The Intimate Motion Picture is an equivalent of the lyric. In the seventeenth chapter it is shown that one type of the Intimate might be classed as imagist. And obviously the Splendor Pictures are the equivalent of the epic.

But perhaps the most adequate way of showing the meaning of this outline is to say that the Action Film is sculpture-in-motion, the Intimate Photoplay is painting-in-motion, and the Fairy Pageant, along with the rest of the Splendor Pictures, may be described as architecture-in-motion. This chapter will discuss the bearing of the phrase sculpture-in-motion. It will relate directly to chapter two.

First, gentle and kindly reader, let us discuss sculpture in its most literal sense; after that, less realistically, but perhaps more ade-

quately. Let us begin with Annette Keller-
man in Neptune's Daughter. This film has
a crude plot constructed to show off Annette's
various athletic resources. It is good photography, and a big idea so far as the swimming
episodes are concerned. An artist haunted
by picture-conceptions equivalent to the
musical thoughts back of Wagner's Rhine-
maidens could have made of Annette, in her
mermaid's dress, a notable figure. Or a story
akin to the mermaid tale of Hans Christian
Andersen, or Matthew Arnold's poem of the
forsaken merman, could have made this picturesque witch of the salt water truly significant,
and still retained the most beautiful parts of
the photoplay as it was exhibited. It is an
exceedingly irrelevant imagination that shows
her in other scenes as a duellist, for instance,
because forsooth she can fence. As a child of
the ocean, half fish, half woman, she is indeed
convincing. Such mermaids as this have
haunted sailors, and lured them on the rocks
to their doom, from the day the siren sang
till the hour the Lorelei sang no more. The
scene with the baby mermaid, when she swims
with the pretty creature on her back, is irresistible. Why are our managers so mechanical?

Why do they flatten out at the moment the fancy of the tiniest reader of fairy-tales begins to be alive? Most of Annette's support were stage dummies. Neptune was a lame Santa Claus with cotton whiskers.

But as for the bearing of the film on this chapter: the human figure is within its rights whenever it is as free from self-consciousness as was the life-radiating Annette in the heavenly clear waters of Bermuda. On the other hand, Neptune and his pasteboard diadem and wooden-pointed pitchfork, should have put on his dressing-gown and retired. As a toe dancer in an alleged court scene, on land, Annette was a mere simperer. Possibly Pavlowa as a swimmer in Bermuda waters would have been as much of a mistake. Each queen to her kingdom.

For living, moving sculpture, the human eye requires a costume and a part in unity with the meaning of that particular figure. There is the Greek dress of Mordkin in the arrow dance. There is Annette's breast covering of shells, and wonderful flowing mermaid hair, clothing her as the midnight does the moon. The new costume freedom of the photoplay allows such limitation of clothing as would be probable when one is honestly in touch with wild nature and preoccupied with vigorous exercise. Thus the cave-man and desert island narratives, though seldom well done, when produced with verisimilitude, give an opportunity for the native human frame in the logical wrappings of reeds and skins. But those who in a silly hurry seek excuses, are generally merely ridiculous, like the barefoot man who is terribly tender about walking on the pebbles, or the wild man who is white as celery or grass under a board. There is no short cut to vitality.

A successful literal use of sculpture is in the film Oil and Water. Blanche Sweet is the leader of the play within a play which occupies the first reel. Here the Olympians and the Muses, with a grace that we fancy was Greek, lead a dance that traces the story of the spring, summer, and autumn of life. Finally the supple dancers turn gray and old and die, but not before they have given us a vision from the Ionian islands. The play might have been inspired from reading Keats' Lamia, but is probably derived from the work of Isadora Duncan. This chapter has hereafter only a passing word or two on literal

sculptural effects. It has more in mind the
carver's attitude toward all that passes before
the eye.

The sculptor George Gray Barnard is responsible for none of the views in this discourse, but he has talked to me at length about
his sense of discovery in watching the most
ordinary motion pictures, and his delight in
following them with their endless combinations
of masses and flowing surfaces.

The little far-away people on the old-
fashioned speaking stage do not appeal to the
plastic sense in this way. They are, by comparison, mere bits of pasteboard with sweet
voices, while, on the other hand, the photoplay
foreground is full of dumb giants. The bodies
of these giants are in high sculptural relief.
Where the lights are quite glaring and the
photography is bad, many of the figures are
as hard in their impact on the eye as lime-
white plaster-casts, no matter what the clothing. There are several passages of this sort
in the otherwise beautiful Enoch Arden, where
the shipwrecked sailor is depicted on his
desert island in the glaring sun.

What materials should the photoplay figures
suggest? There are as many possible materials

as there are subjects for pictures and tone schemes to be considered. But we will take for illustration wood, bronze, and marble, since they have been used in the old sculptural art.

There is found in most art shows a type of carved wood gargoyle where the work and the subject are at one, not only in the color of the wood, but in the way the material masses itself, in bulk betrays its qualities. We will suppose a moving picture humorist who is in the same mood as the carver. He chooses a story of quaint old ladies, street gamins, and fat aldermen. Imagine the figures with the same massing and interplay suddenly invested with life, yet giving to the eye a pleasure kindred to that which is found in carved wood, and bringing to the fancy a similar humor.

Or there is a type of Action Story where the mood of the figures is that of bronze, with the æsthetic resources of that metal: its elasticity; its emphasis on the tendon, ligament, and bone, rather than on the muscle; and an attribute that we will call the panther-like quality. Hermon A. MacNeil has a memorable piece of work in the yard of the architect Shaw, at Lake Forest, Illinois. It is called "The Sun Vow."

A little Indian is shooting toward the sun, while the old warrior, crouching immediately behind him, follows with his eye the direction of the arrow. Few pieces of sculpture come readily to mind that show more happily the qualities of bronze as distinguished from other materials. To imagine such a group done in marble, carved wood, or Della Robbia ware is to destroy the very image in the fancy.

The photoplay of the American Indian should in most instances be planned as bronze in action. The tribes should not move so rapidly that the panther-like elasticity is lost in the riding, running, and scalping. On the other hand, the aborigines should be far from the temperateness of marble.

Mr. Edward S. Curtis, the super-photographer, has made an Ethnological collection of photographs of our American Indians. This work of a life-time, a supreme art achievement, shows the native as a figure in bronze. Mr. Curtis' photoplay, The Land of the Head Hunters (World Film Corporation), a romance of the Indians of the North-West, abounds in noble bronzes.

I have gone through my old territories as an art student, in the Chicago Art Institute and

the Metropolitan Museum, of late, in special
excursions, looking for sculpture, painting, and
architecture that might be the basis for the
photoplays of the future.

The Bacchante of Frederick MacMonnies is
in bronze in the Metropolitan Museum and in
bronze replica in the Boston Museum of Fine
Arts.   There is probably no work that more
rejoices the hearts of the young art students in
either city.   The youthful creature illustrates
a most joyous leap into the air.   She is high on
one foot with the other knee lifted.   She holds
a bunch of grapes full-arm's length.   Her baby,
clutched in the other hand, is reaching up with
greedy mouth toward the fruit.   The bacchante
body is glistening in the light.   This is joy-in-
bronze as the Sun Vow is power-in-bronze.
This special story could not be told in another
medium.   I have seen in Paris a marble copy
of this Bacchante.   It is as though it were
done in soap.   On the other hand, many of the
renaissance Italian sculptors have given us
children in marble in low relief, dancing like
lilies in the wind.   They could not be put into
bronze.

The plot of the Action Photoplay is literally
or metaphorically a chase down the road or a

hurdle-race.   It might be well to consider how typical figures for such have been put into carved material.   There are two bronze statues that have their replicas in all museums.   They are generally one on either side of the main hall, towering above the second-story balustrade. First, the statue of Gattamelata, a Venetian general, by Donatello.   The original is in Padua.   Then there is the figure of Bartolommeo Colleoni.   The original is in Venice. It is by Verrocchio and Leopardi.   These equestrians radiate authority.   There is more action in them than in any cowboy hordes I have ever beheld zipping across the screen. Look upon them and ponder long, prospective author-producer.   Even in a simple chase-picture, the speed must not destroy the chance to enjoy the modelling.   If you would give us mounted legions, destined to conquer, let any one section of the film, if it is stopped and studied, be grounded in the same bronze conception.   The Assyrian commanders in Griffith's Judith would, without great embarrassment, stand this test.

But it may not be the pursuit of an enemy we have in mind.   It may be a spring celebration, horsemen in Arcadia, going to some

happy tournament. Where will we find our
precedents for such a cavalcade? Go to any
museum. Find the Parthenon room. High
on the wall is the copy of the famous marble
frieze of the young citizens who are in the procession in praise of Athena. Such a rhythm
of bodies and heads and the feet of proud steeds,
and above all the profiles of thoroughbred
youths, no city has seen since that day. The
delicate composition relations, ever varying,
ever refreshing, amid the seeming sameness of
formula of rider behind rider, have been the
delight of art students the world over, and shall
so remain. No serious observer escapes the
exhilaration of this company. Let it be studied
by the author-producer though it be but an
idyl in disguise that his scenario calls for:
merry young farmers hurrying to the State
Fair parade, boys making all speed to the
political rally.

Buy any three moving picture magazines
you please. Mark the illustrations that are
massive, in high relief, with long lines in their
edges. Cut out and sort some of these. I
have done it on the table where I write. · After
throwing away all but the best specimens, I
have four different kinds of sculpture. First,

behold the inevitable cowboy. He is on a ramping horse, filling the entire outlook. The steed rears, while facing us. The cowboy waves his hat. There is quite such an animal by Frederick MacMonnies, wrought in bronze, set up on a gate to a park in Brooklyn. It is not the identical color of the photoplay animal, but the bronze elasticity is the joy in both.

Here is a scene of a masked monk, carrying off a fainting girl. The hero intercepts him. The figures of the lady and the monk are in sufficient sculptural harmony to make a formal sculptural group for an art exhibition. The picture of the hero, strong, with well-massed surfaces, is related to both. The fact that he is in evening dress does not alter his monumental quality. All three are on a stone balcony that relates itself to the general largeness of spirit in the group, and the semi-classic dress of the maiden. No doubt the title is: The Morning Following the Masquerade Ball. This group could be made in unglazed clay, in four colors.

Here is an American lieutenant with two ladies. The three are suddenly alert over the approach of the villain, who is not yet in the

picture.   In costume it is an everyday group,
but those three figures are related to one another, and the trees behind them, in simple
sculptural terms.   The lieutenant, as is to be
expected, looks forth in fierce readiness.   One
girl stands with clasped hands.   The other
points to the danger.   The relations of these
people to one another may seem merely dramatic
to the superficial observer, but the power of the
group is in the fact that it is monumental.   I
could imagine it done in four different kinds
of rare tropical wood, carved unpolished.

Here is a scene of storm and stress in an office
where the hero is caught with seemingly in-
criminating papers.   The table is in confusion.
The room is filling with people, led by one
accusing woman.   Is this also sculpture?   Yes.
The figures are in high relief.   Even the surfaces
of the chairs and the littered table are massive,
and the eye travels without weariness, as it
should do in sculpture, from the hero to the furious woman, then to the attorney behind her,
then to the two other revilers, then to the crowd
in three loose rhythmic ranks.   The eye makes
this journey, not from space to space, or fabric to
fabric, but first of all from mass to mass.   It
is sculpture, but it is the sort that can be done

in no medium but the moving picture itself, and therefore it is one goal of this argument.

But there are several other goals. One of the sculpturesque resources of the photoplay is that the human countenance can be magnified many times, till it fills the entire screen. Some examples are in rather low relief, portraits approximating certain painters. But if they are on sculptural terms, and are studies of the faces of thinking men, let the producer make a pilgrimage to Washington for his precedent. There, in the rotunda of the capitol, is the face of Lincoln by Gutzon Borglum. It is one of the eminently successful attempts to get at the secret of the countenance by enlarging it much, and concentrating the whole consideration there.

The photoplay producer, seemingly without taking thought, is apt to show a sculptural sense in giving us Newfoundland fishermen, clad in oilskins. The background may have an unconscious Winslow Homer reminiscence. In the foreground our hardy heroes fill the screen, and dripping with sea-water become wave-beaten granite, yet living creatures none the less. Imagine some one chapter from the story of Little Em'ly in David Copperfield, retold in the films. Show us Ham Peggotty

and old Mr. Peggotty in colloquy over their
nets.   There are many powerful bronze groups
to be had from these two, on to the heroic and
unselfish death of Ham, rescuing his enemy in
storm and lightning.

I have seen one rich picture of alleged canni-
bal tribes.   It was a comedy about a missionary.
But the aborigines were like living ebony and
silver.   That was long ago.   Such things come
too much by accident.   The producer is not
sufficiently aware that any artistic element in
his list of productions that is allowed to go wild,
that has not had full analysis, reanalysis, and
final conservation, wastes his chance to attain
supreme mastery.

Open your history of sculpture, and dwell
upon those illustrations which are not the normal, reposeful statues, but the exceptional,
such as have been listed for this chapter.
Imagine that each dancing, galloping, or fighting figure comes down into the room life-size.
Watch it against a dark curtain.   Let it go
through a series of gestures in harmony with
the spirit of the original conception, and as
rapidly as possible, not to lose nobility.   If
you have the necessary elasticity, imagine
the figures wearing the costumes of another

period, yet retaining in their motions the same
essential spirit. Combine them in your mind
with one or two kindred figures, enlarged till
they fill the end of the room. You have now
created the beginning of an Action Photoplay in
your own fancy.

Do this with each most energetic classic till
your imagination flags. I do not want to be
too dogmatic, but it seems to me this is one
way to evolve real Action Plays. It would,
perhaps, be well to substitute this for the usual
method of evolving them from old stage material or newspaper clippings.

There is in the Metropolitan Museum a
noble modern group, the Mares of Diomedes,
by the aforementioned Gutzon Borglum. It
is full of material for the meditations of a man
who wants to make a film of a stampede.
The idea is that Hercules, riding his steed bare-
back, guides it in a circle. He is fascinating the
horses he has been told to capture. They are
held by the mesmerism of the circular path
and follow him round and round till they finally
fall from exhaustion. Thus the Indians of the
West capture wild ponies, and Borglum, a far
western man, imputes the method to Hercules.
The bronze group shows a segment of this

circle. The whirlwind is at its height. The mares are wild to taste the flesh of Hercules. Whoever is to photograph horses, let him study the play of light and color and muscle-texture in this bronze. And let no group of horses ever run faster than these of Borglum.

An occasional hint of a Michelangelo figure or gesture appears for a flash in the films. Young artist in the audience, does it pass you by? Open your history of sculpture again and look at the usual list of Michelangelo groups. Suppose the seated majesty of Moses should rise, what would be the quality of the action? Suppose the sleeping figures of the Medician tombs should wake, or those famous slaves should break their bands, or David again hurl the stone. Would not their action be as heroic as their quietness? Is it not possible to have a Michelangelo of photoplay sculpture? Should we not look for him in the fulness of time? His figures might come to us in the skins of the desert island solitary, or as cave men and women, or as mermaids and mermen, and yet have a force and grandeur akin to that of the old Italian.

Rodin's famous group of the citizens of Calais is an example of the expression of one particular idea by a special technical treatment. The producer who tells a kindred story to that of the siege of Calais, and the final going of these humble men to their doom, will have a hero-tale indeed. It will be not only sculpture-in-action, but a great Crowd Picture. It begins to be seen that the possibilities of monumental achievement in the films transcend the narrow boundaries of the Action Photoplay. Why not conceptions as heroic as Rodin's Hand of God, where the first pair are clasped in the gigantic fingers of their maker in the clay from which they came?

Finally, I desire in moving pictures, not the stillness, but the majesty of sculpture. I do not advocate for the photoplay the mood of the Venus of Milo. But let us turn to that sister of hers, the great Victory of Samothrace, that spreads her wings at the head of the steps of the Louvre, and in many an art gallery beside. When you are appraising a new film, ask yourself: "Is this motion as rapid, as godlike, as the sweep of the wings of the Samothracian?" Let her be the touchstone of the Action Drama, for nothing can be more swift than the winged Gods, nothing can be more powerful than the oncoming of the immortals.

CHAPTER IX

PAINTING-IN-MOTION

THIS chapter is founded on the delicate effects that may be worked out from cosy interior scenes, close to the camera. It relates directly to chapter three.

While the Intimate-and-friendly Motion Picture may be in high sculptural relief, its characteristic manifestations are in low relief. The situations show to better advantage when they seem to be paintings rather than monumental groups.

Turn to your handful of motion picture magazines and mark the illustrations that look the most like paintings. Cut them out. Winnow them several times. I have before me, as a final threshing from such an experiment, five pictures. Each one approximates a different school.

Here is a colonial Virginia maiden by the hearth of the inn. Bending over her in a cherishing way is the negro maid. On the

other side, the innkeeper shows a kindred solici-
tude. A dishevelled traveller sleeps huddled
up in the corner. The costume of the man
fades into the velvety shadows of the wall.
His face is concealed. His hair blends with
the soft background. The clothing of the other
three makes a patch of light gray. Added to
this is the gayety of special textures: the
turban of the negress, a trimming on the skirt
of the heroine, the silkiness of the innkeeper's
locks, the fabric of the broom in the hearth-
light, the pattern of the mortar lines round the
bricks of the hearth. The tableau is a satisfying scheme in two planes and many textures.

Here is another sort of painting. The young
mother in her pretty bed is smiling on her
infant. The cot and covers and flesh tints
have gentle scales of difference, all within one
tone of the softest gray. Her hair is quite
dark. It relates to the less luminous black of
the coat of the physician behind the bed and the
dress of the girl-friend bending over her. The
nurse standing by the doctor is a figure of the
same gray-white as the bed. Within the pattern of the velvety-blacks there are as many
subtle gradations as in the pattern of the
gray-whites. The tableau is a satisfying

scheme in black and gray, with practically one non-obtrusive texture throughout.

Here is a picture of an Englishman and his wife, in India. It might be called sculptural, but for the magnificence of the turban of the rajah who converses with them, the glitter of the light round his shoulders, and the scheme of shadow out of which the three figures rise. The arrangement remotely reminds one of several of Rembrandt's semi-oriental musings.

Here is a picture of Mary Pickford as Fanchon the Cricket. She is in the cottage with the strange old mother. I have seen a painting in this mood by the Greek Nickolas Gysis.

The Intimate-and-friendly Moving Picture, the photoplay of painting-in-motion, need not be indoors as long as it has the native-heath mood. It is generally keyed to the hearth-stone, and keeps quite close to it. But how well I remember when the first French photoplays began to come. Though unintelligent in some respects, the photography and subject-matter of many of them made one think of that painter of gentle out-of-door scenes, Jean Charles Cazin. Here is our last clipping, which is also in a spirit allied to Cazin. The heroine, accompanied by an aged shepherd

and his dog, are in the foreground. The sheep
are in the middle distance on the edge of the
river. There is a noble hill beyond the gently
flowing water. Here is intimacy and friendliness in the midst of the big out of doors.

If these five photo-paintings were on good
paper enlarged to twenty by twenty-four inches,
they would do to frame and hang on the wall
of any study, for a month or so. And after the
relentless test of time, I would venture that
some one of the five would prove a permanent
addition to the household gods.

Hastily made photographs selected from the
films are often put in front of the better theatres
to advertise the show. Of late they are making
them two by three feet and sometimes several
times larger. Here is a commercial beginning
of an art gallery, but not enough pains are
taken to give the selections a complete art
gallery dignity. Why not have the most beautiful scenes in front of the theatres, instead
of those alleged to be the most thrilling? Why
not rest the fevered and wandering eye, rather
than make one more attempt to take it by force?

Let the reader supply another side of the
argument by looking at the illustrations in
any history of painting. Let him select the

pictures' that charm him most, and think of them enlarged and transferred bodily to one corner of the room, as he has thought of the sculpture. Let them take on motion without losing their charm of low relief, or their serene composition within the four walls of the frame. As for the motion, let it be a further extension of the drawing. Let every gesture be a bolder but not less graceful brush-stroke.

The Metropolitan Museum has a Van Dyck that appeals equally to one's sense of beauty and one's feeling for humor. It is a portrait of James Stuart, Duke of Lennox, and I cannot see how the author-producer-photographer can look upon it without having it set his imagination in a glow. Every small town dancing set has a James like this. The man and the greyhound are the same witless breed, the kind that achieve a result by their clean-limbed elegance alone. Van Dyck has painted the two with what might be called a greyhound brush-stroke, a style of handling that is nothing but courtly convention and strut to the point of genius. He is as far from the meditative spirituality of Rembrandt as could well be imagined.

Conjure up a scene in the hereditary hall

after a hunt (or golf tournament), in which a man like this Duke of Lennox has a noble parley with his lady (or dancing partner), she being a sweet and stupid swan (or a white rabbit) by the same sign that he is a noble and stupid greyhound. Be it an ancient or modern episode, the story could be told in the tone and with well-nigh the brushwork of Van Dyck.

Then there is a picture my teachers, Chase and Henri, were never weary of praising, the Girl with the Parrot, by Manet. Here continence in nervous force, expressed by low relief and restraint in tone, is carried to its ultimate point. I should call this an imagist painting, made before there were such people as imagist poets. It is a perpetual sermon to those that would thresh around to no avail, be they orators, melodramatists, or makers of photoplays with an alleged heart-interest.

Let us consider Gilbert Stuart's portrait of Washington. This painter's notion of personal dignity has far more of the intellectual quality than Van Dyck. He loves to give us stately, able, fairly conscientious gentry, rather than overdone royalty. His work represents a certain mood in design that in architecture is called colonial. Such portraits go with houses like Mount Vernon. Let the photographer study the flat blacks in the garments. Let him note the transparent impression of the laces and flesh-tints that seem to be painted on glass, observing especially the crystalline whiteness of the wigs. Let him inspect also the silhouette-like outlines, noting the courtly self-possession they convey. Then let the photographer, the producer, and the author, be they one man or six men, stick to this type of picturization through one entire production, till any artist in the audience will say, "This photoplay was painted by a pupil of Gilbert Stuart"; and the layman will say, "It looks like those stately days." And let us not have battle, but a Mount Vernon fireside tale.

Both the Chicago and New York museums contain many phases of one same family group, painted by George de Forest Brush. There is a touch of the hearthstone priestess about the woman. The force of sex has turned to the austere comforting passion of mother-hood. From the children, under the wings of this spirit, come special delicate powers of life. There is nothing tense or restless about them, yet they embody action, the beating of the inner fire, without which all outer action is mockery. Hearthstone tales keyed to the mood and using the brush stroke that delineates this especial circle would be unmistakable in their distinction.

Charles W. Hawthorne has pictures in Chicago and New York that imply the Intimate-and-friendly Photoplay. The Trousseau in the Metropolitan Museum shows a gentle girl, an unfashionable home-body with a sweetly sheltered air. Behind her glimmers the patient mother's face. The older woman is busy about fitting the dress. The picture is a tribute to the qualities of many unknown gentlewomen. Such an illumination as this, on faces so innocently eloquent, is the light that should shine on the countenance of the photoplay actress who really desires greatness in the field of the Intimate Motion Picture. There is in Chicago, Hawthorne's painting of Sylvia: a little girl standing with her back to a mirror, a few blossoms in one hand and a vase of flowers on the mirror shelf. It is as sound a composition as Hawthorne ever produced. The painting of the child is another tribute to the physical-spiritual textures from which humanity is made. Ah, you producer who have grown squeaky whipping your people into what you

called action, consider the dynamics of these
figures that would be almost motionless in
real life.   Remember there must be a spirit-
action under the other, or all is dead.

Yet that soul may be the muse of Comedy.
If Hawthorne and his kind are not your fashion,
turn to models that have their feet on the
earth always, yet successfully aspire.   Key
some of your intimate humorous scenes to
the Dutch Little Masters of Painting, such
pictures as Gerard Terburg's Music Lesson in
the Chicago Art Institute.   The thing is as
well designed as a Dutch house, wind-mill, or
clock.   And it is more elegant than any of
these.   There is humor enough in the picture
to last one reel through.   The society dame
of the period, in her pretty raiment, fingers the
strings of her musical instrument, while the
master stands by her with the baton.   The
painter has enjoyed the satire, from her elegant
little hands to the teacher's well-combed locks.
It is very plain that she does not want to study
music with any sincerity, and he does not
desire to develop the ability of this particular
person.   There may be a flirtation in the background.   Yet these people are not hollow as
gourds, and they are not caricatured.   The

Dutch Little Masters have indulged in numberless characterizations of mundane humanity.
But they are never so preoccupied with the
story that it is an anecdote rather than a
picture. It is, first of all, a piece of elegant
painting-fabric. Next it is a scrap of Dutch
philosophy or aspiration.

Let Whistler turn over in his grave while
we enlist him for the cause of democracy. One
view of the technique of this man might
summarize it thus: fastidiousness in choice
of subject, the picture well within the frame,
low relief, a Velasquez study of tones and a
Japanese study of spaces. Let us, dear and
patient reader, particularly dwell upon the
spacing. A Whistler, or a good Japanese
print, might be described as a kaleidoscope
suddenly arrested and transfixed at the moment
of most exquisite relations in the pieces of glass.
An Intimate Play of a kindred sort would
start to turning the kaleidoscope again, losing
fine relations only to gain those which are more
exquisite and novel. All motion pictures might
be characterized as *space measured without
sound, plus time measured without sound.*
This description fits in a special way the delicate form of the Intimate Motion Picture,

and there can be studied out, free from irrelevant issues.

As to *space measured without sound.* Suppose it is a humorous characterization of comfortable family life, founded on some Dutch Little Master. The picture measures off its spaces in harmony. The triangle occupied by the little child's dress is in definite relation to the triangle occupied by the mother's costume. To these two patterns the space measured off by the boy's figure is adjusted, and all of them are as carefully related to the shapes cut out of the background by the figures. No matter how the characters move about in the photoplay, these pattern shapes should relate to one another in a definite design. The exact tone value of each one and their precise nearness or distance to one another have a deal to do with the final effect.

We go to the photoplay to enjoy right and splendid picture-motions, to feel a certain thrill when the pieces of kaleidoscope glass slide into new places. Instead of moving on straight lines, as they do in the mechanical toy, they progress in strange curves that are part of the very shapes into which they fall.

Consider: first came the photograph. Then

motion was added to the photograph. We must use this order in our judgment. If it is ever to evolve into a national art, it must first be good picture, then good motion.

Belasco's attitude toward the stage has been denounced by the purists because he makes settings too large a portion of his story-telling, and transforms his theatre into the paradise of the property-man. But this very quality of the well spaced setting, if you please, has made his chance for the world's moving picture anthology. As reproduced by Jesse K. Lasky the Belasco production is the only type of the old-line drama that seems really made to be the basis of a moving picture play. Not always, but as a general rule, Belasco suffers less detriment in the films than other men. Take, for instance, the Belasco-Lasky production of The Rose of the Rancho with Bessie Barriscale as the heroine. It has many highly modelled action-tableaus, and others that come under the classification of this chapter. When I was attending it not long ago, here in my home town, the fair companion at my side said that one scene looked like a painting by Sorolla y Bastida, the Spaniard. It is the episode where the Rose sends back her servant to inquire

the hero's name. As a matter of fact there
were Sorollas and Zuloagas all through the
piece. The betrothal reception with flying
confetti was a satisfying piece of Spanish splendor. It was space music indeed, space
measured without sound. Incidentally the
cast is to be congratulated on its picturesque
acting, especially Miss Barriscale in her impersonation of the Rose.

It is harder to grasp the other side of the
paradox, picture-motions considered as *time
measured without sound.* But think of a
lively and humoresque clock that does not tick
and takes only an hour to record a day.   Think
of a noiseless electric vehicle, where you are
looking out of the windows, going down the
smooth boulevard of Wonderland. Consider
a film with three simple time-elements : (1)
that of the pursuer, (2) the pursued, (3) the
observation vehicle of the camera following
the road and watching both of them, now
faster, now slower than they, as the photographer overtakes the actors or allows them to
hurry ahead. The plain chase is a bore because there are only these three time-elements.
But the chase principle survives in every
motion picture and we simply need more of this

sort of time measurement, better considered. The more the non-human objects, the human actors, and the observer move at a varying pace, the greater chances there are for what might be called time-and-space music.

No two people in the same room should gesture at one mechanical rate, or lift their forks or spoons, keeping obviously together. Yet it stands to reason that each successive tableau should be not only a charming picture, but the totals of motion should be an orchestration of various speeds, of abrupt, graceful, and seemingly awkward progress, worked into a silent symphony.

Supposing it is a fisher-maiden's romance. In the background the waves toss in one tempo. Owing to the sail, the boat rocks in another. In the foreground the tree alternately bends and recovers itself in the breeze, making more opposition than the sail. In still another time-unit the smoke rolls from the chimney, making no resistance to the wind. In another unit, the lovers pace the sand. Yet there is one least common multiple in which all move. This the producing genius should sense and make part of the dramatic structure, and it would have its bearing on the

periodic appearance of the minor and major
crises.

Films like this, you say, would be hard to
make. Yes. Here is the place to affirm that
the one-reel Intimate Photoplay will no doubt
be the form in which this type of time-and-
space music is developed. The music of silent
motion is the most abstract of moving picture
attributes and will probably remain the least
comprehended. Like the quality of Walter
Pater's Marius the Epicurean, or that of
Shelley's Hymn to Intellectual Beauty, it will
not satisfy the sudden and the brash.

The reader will find in his round of the picture theatres many single scenes and parts of
plays that elucidate the title of this chapter.
Often the first two-thirds of the story will fit
it well. Then the producers, finding that, for
reasons they do not understand, with the best
and most earnest actors they cannot work the
three reels into an emotional climax, introduce
some stupid disaster and rescue utterly irrelevant to the character-parts and the paintings that have preceded. Whether the alleged
thesis be love, hate, or ambition, cottage charm,
daisy dell sweetness, or the ivy beauty of an

ancient estate, the resource for the final punch seems to be something like a train-wreck. But the transfiguration of the actors, not their destruction or rescue, is the goal. The last moment of the play is great, not when it is a grandiose salvation from a burning house, that knocks every delicate preceding idea in the head, but a tableau that is as logical as the awakening of the Sleeping Beauty after the hero has explored all the charmed castle.

CHAPTER X

THE Action Pictures are sculpture-in-motion, the Intimate Pictures, paintings-in-motion, the Splendor Pictures, many and diverse. It seems far-fetched, perhaps, to complete the analogy and say they are architecture-in-motion; yet, patient reader, unless I am mistaken, that assumption can be given a value in time without straining your imagination.

Landscape gardening, mural painting, church building, and furniture making as well, are some of the things that come under the head of architecture. They are discussed between the covers of any architectural magazine. There is a particular relation in the photoplay between Crowd Pictures and landscape conceptions, between Patriotic Films and mural paintings, between Religious Films and architecture. And there is just as much of a relation between Fairy Tales and furniture, which same is discussed in this chapter.

Let us return to Moving Day, chapter four.
This idea has been represented many times with
a certain sameness because the producers have
not thought out the philosophy behind it. A
picture that is all action is a plague, one that
is all elephantine and pachydermatous pageant
is a bore, and, most emphatically, a film that
is all mechanical legerdemain is a nuisance.
The possible charm in a so-called trick picture
is in eliminating the tricks, giving them dignity
till they are no longer such, but thoughts in
motion and made visible. In Moving Day the
shoes are the most potent. They go through a
drama that is natural to them. To march without human feet inside is but to exaggerate themselves. It would not be amusing to have them
walk upside down, for instance. As long as
the worn soles touch the pavement, we unconsciously conjure up the character of the
absent owners, about whom the shoes are
indeed gossiping. So let the remainder of the
furniture keep still while the shoes do their
best. Let us call to mind a classic fairy-tale
involving shoes that are magical: The Seven
Leagued Boots, for example, or The Enchanted
Moccasins, or the footwear of Puss in Boots.
How gorgeous and embroidered any of these

should be, and at a crisis what sly antics they
should be brought to play, without fidgeting
all over the shop! Cinderella's Slipper is
not sufficiently the heroine in moving pictures
of that story. It should be the tiny leading
lady of the piece, in the same sense the mighty
steam-engine is the hero of the story in chapter
two. The peasants when they used to tell the
tale by the hearth fire said the shoe was made
of glass. This was in mediæval Europe, at a
time when glass was much more of a rarity.
The material was chosen to imply a sort of
jewelled strangeness from the start. When
Cinderella loses it in her haste, it should flee
at once like a white mouse, to hide under
the sofa. It should be pictured there with
special artifice, so that the sensuous little foot
of every girl-child in the audience will tingle
to wear it. It should move a bit when the
prince comes frantically hunting his lady, and
peep out just in time for that royal per-
sonage to spy it. Even at the coronation it
should be the centre of the ritual, more gazed
at than the crown, and on as dazzling a
cushion. The final taking on of the slipper
by the lady should be as stately a ceremony
as the putting of the circlet of gold on her

aureole hair. So much for Cinderella. But there are novel stories that should be evolved by preference, about new sorts of magic shoes.

We have not exhausted Moving Day. The chairs kept still through the Cinderella discourse. Now let them take their innings. Instead of having all of them dance about, invest but one with an inner life. Let its special attributes show themselves but gradually, reaching their climax at the highest point of excitement in the reel, and being an integral part of that enthusiasm. Perhaps, though we be inventing a new fairy-tale, it will resemble the Siege Perilous in the Arthurian story, the chair where none but the perfect knight could sit. A dim row of flaming swords might surround it. When the soul entitled to use this throne appears, the swords might fade away and the gray cover hanging in slack folds roll back because of an inner energy and the chair might turn from gray to white, and with a subtle change of line become a throne.

The photoplay imagination which is able to impart vital individuality to furniture will not stop there. Let the buildings emanate conscious life. The author-producer-photog-

rapher, or one or all three, will make into a
personality some place akin to the House of the
Seven Gables till the ancient building dominates
the fancy as it does in Hawthorne's tale.   There
are various ways to bring about this result :
by having its outlines waver in the twilight,
by touches of phosphorescence, or by the passing of inexplicable shadows or the like.   It
depends upon what might be called the genius
of the building.   There is the Poe story of The
Fall of the House of Usher, where with the
death of the last heir the castle falls crumbling
into the tarn.   There are other possible tales
on such terms, never yet imagined, to be born
tomorrow.   Great structures may become in
sort villains, as in the old Bible narrative of
the origin of the various languages.   The producer can show the impious Babel Tower, going
higher and higher into the sky, fascinating and
tempting the architects till a confusion of
tongues turns those masons into quarrelling
mobs that become departing caravans, leaving
her blasted and forsaken, a symbol of every
Babylon that rose after her.

There are fables where the rocks and the
mountains speak.   Emerson has given us one
where the Mountain and the Squirrel had a

quarrel. The Mountain called the Squirrel "Little Prig." And then continues a clash of personalities more possible to illustrate than at first appears. Here we come to the second stage of the fairy-tale where the creature seems so unmanageable in his physical aspect that some actor must be substituted who will embody the essence of him. To properly illustrate the quarrel of the Mountain and the Squirrel, the steep height should quiver and heave and then give forth its personality in the figure of a vague smoky giant, capable of human argument, but with oak-roots in his hair, and Bun, perhaps, become a jester in squirrel's dress.

Or it may be our subject matter is a tall Dutch clock. Father Time himself might emerge therefrom. Or supposing it is a chapel, in a knight's adventure. An angel should step from the carving by the door : a design that is half angel, half flower. But let the clock first tremble a bit. Let the carving stir a little, and then let the spirit come forth, that there may be a fine relation between the impersonator and the thing represented. A statue too often takes on life by having the actor abruptly substituted. The actor cannot logically take on more personality than the statue has.   He can only give that personality expression in a new channel.   In the realm of letters, a real transformation scene, rendered credible to the higher fancy by its slow cumulative movement, is the tale of the change of the dying Rowena to the living triumphant Ligeia in Poe's story of that name.   Substitution is not the fairy-story.   It is transformation, transfiguration, that is the fairy-story, be it a divine or a diabolical change.   There is never more than one witch in a forest, one Siege Perilous at any Round Table.   But she is indeed a witch and the other is surely a Siege Perilous.

We might define Fairy Splendor as furniture transfigured, for without transfiguration there is no spiritual motion of any kind.   But the phrase "furniture-in-motion" serves a purpose. It gets us back to the earth for a reason. Furniture is architecture, and the fairy-tale picture should certainly be drawn with architectural lines.   The normal fairy-tale is a sort of tiny informal child's religion, the baby's secular temple, and it should have for the most part that touch of delicate sublimity that we see in the mountain chapel or grotto, or fancy in the dwellings of Aucassin and Nicolette.

When such lines are drawn by the truly sophisticated producer, there lies in them the secret of a more than ritualistic power. Good fairy architecture amounts to an incantation in itself.

If it is a grown-up legend, it must be more than monumental in its lines, like the great stone face of Hawthorne's tale. Even a chair can reach this estate. For instance, let it be the throne of Wodin, illustrating some passage in Norse mythology. If this throne has a language, it speaks with the lightning; if it shakes with its threat, it moves the entire mountain range beneath it. Let the wizard-author-producer climb up from the tricks of Moving Day to the foot-hills where he can see this throne against the sky, as a superarchitect would draw it. But even if he can give this vision in the films, his task will not be worth while if he is simply a teller of old stories. Let us have magic shoes about which are more golden dreams than those concerning Cinderella. Let us have stranger castles than that of Usher, more dazzling chairs than the Siege Perilous. Let us have the throne of Liberty, not the throne of Wodin.

There is one outstanding photoplay that I always have in mind when I think of film magic. It illustrates some principles of this chapter and chapter four, as well as many others through the book. It is Griffith's production of The Avenging Conscience. It is also an example of that rare thing, a use of old material that is so inspired that it has the dignity of a new creation. The raw stuff of the plot is pieced together from the story of The Telltale Heart and the poem Annabel Lee. It has behind it, in the further distance, Poe's conscience stories of The Black Cat, and William Wilson. I will describe the film here at length, and apply it to whatever chapters it illustrates.

An austere and cranky bachelor (well impersonated by Spottiswoode Aitken) brings up his orphan nephew with an awkward affection. The nephew is impersonated by Henry B. Walthall. The uncle has an ambition that the boy will become a man of letters. In his attempts at literature the youth is influenced by Poe. This brings about the Poe quality of his dreams at the crisis. The uncle is silently exasperated when he sees his boy's writing-time broken into, and wasted, as he thinks, by an affair with a lovely Annabel (Blanche Sweet). The intimacy and confidence of the lovers has progressed so far that it is a natural

thing for the artless girl to cross the gardens
and after hesitation knock at the door. She
wants to know what has delayed her boy.
She is all in a flutter on account of the overdue
appointment to go to a party together. The
scene of the pretty hesitancy on the step, her
knocking, and the final impatient tapping with
her foot is one of the best illustrations of the
intimate mood in photoplay episodes. On the
girl's entrance the uncle overwhelms her and
the boy by saying she is pursuing his nephew
like a common woman of the town. The words
actually burst through the film, not as a melodramatic, but as an actual insult. This is a
thing almost impossible to do in the photoplay. This outrage in the midst of an
atmosphere of chivalry is one of Griffith's
master-moments. It accounts for the vol-
canic fury of the nephew that takes such trouble
to burn itself out afterwards. It is not easy
for the young to learn that they must let those
people flay them for an hour who have made
every sacrifice for them through a lifetime.

This scene of insult and the confession scene,
later in this film, moved me as similar passages
in high drama would do ; and their very rareness,
even in the hands of photoplay masters, indicates

that such purely dramatic climaxes cannot be the main asset of the moving picture.   Over and over, with the best talent and producers, they fail.

The boy and girl go to the party in spite of the uncle.   It is while on the way that the boy looks on the face of a stranger who afterwards mixes up in his dream as the detective.   There is a mistake in the printing here.   There are several minutes of a worldly-wise oriental dance to amuse the guests, while the lovers are alone at another end of the garden.   It is, possibly, the aptest contrast with the seriousness of our hero and heroine.   But the social affair could have had a better title than the one that is printed on the film "An Old-fashioned Sweetheart Party."   Possibly the dance was put in after the title.

The lovers part forever.   The girl's pride has had a mortal wound.   About this time is thrown on the screen the kind of a climax quite surely possible to the photoplay.   It reminds one, not of the mood of Poe's verse, but of the spirit of the paintings of George Frederick Watts.   It is allied in some way, in my mind, with his "Love and Life," though but a single draped figure within doors, and

"Love and Life " are undraped figures, climbing a mountain.

The boy, having said good-by, remembers the lady Annabel. It is a crisis after the event. In his vision she is shown in a darkened passageway, all in white, looking out of the window upon the moonlit sky. Simple enough in its elements, this vision is shown twice in glory. The third replica has not the same glamour. The first two are transfigurations into divinity. The phrase thrown on the screen is "The moon never beams without bringing me dreams of the beautiful Annabel Lee." And the sense of loss goes through and through one like a flight of arrows. Another noble picture, more realistic, more sculpturesque, is of Annabel mourning on her knees in her room. Her bended head makes her akin to "Niobe, all tears."

The boy meditating on a park-path is meanwhile watching the spider in his web devour the fly. Then he sees the ants in turn destroy the spider. These pictures are shown on so large a scale that the spiderweb fills the end of the theatre. Then the ant-tragedy does the same. They can be classed as particularly apt hieroglyphics in the sense of chapter thirteen.

Their horror and decorative iridescence are of the Poe sort. It is the first hint of the Poe hieroglyphic we have had except the black patch over the eye of the uncle, along with his jaundiced, cadaverous face. The boy meditates on how all nature turns on cruelty and the survival of the fittest.

He passes just now an Italian laborer (impersonated by George Seigmann). This laborer enters later into his dream. He finally goes to sleep in his chair, the resolve to kill his uncle rankling in his heart.

The audience is not told that a dream begins. To understand that, one must see the film through twice. But it is perfectly legitimate to deceive us. Through our ignorance we share the young man's hallucinations, entering into them as imperceptibly as he does. We think it is the next morning. Poe would start the story just here, and here the veritable Poe-esque quality begins.

After debate within himself as to means, the nephew murders his uncle and buries him in the thick wall of the chimney. The Italian laborer witnesses the death-struggle through the window. While our consciences are aching and the world crashes round us, he levies blackmail. Then for due compensation the Italian becomes an armed sentinel. The boy fears detection.

Yet the foolish youth thinks he will be happy. But every time he runs to meet his sweetheart he is appalled by hallucinations over her shoulder. The cadaverous ghost of the uncle is shown on the screen several times. It is an appearance visible to the young man and the audience only. Later the ghost is implied by the actions of the guilty one. We merely imagine it. This is a piece of sound technique. We no more need a dray full of ghosts than a dray full of jumping furniture.

The village in general has never suspected the nephew. Only two people suspect him: the broken-hearted girl and an old friend of his father. This gentleman puts a detective on the trail. (The detective is impersonated by Ralph Lewis.) The gradual breakdown of the victim is traced by dramatic degrees. This is the second case of the thing I have argued as being generally impossible in a photoplay chronicle of a private person, and which the considerations of chapter twelve indicate as exceptional. We trace the innermost psychology of one special citizen step by step to the crisis, and that path is actually the primary interest of the story. The climax is the confession to the detective. With this self-exposure the direct Poe-quality of the technique comes to an end.   Moreover, Poe would end the story here.   But the Poe-dream is set like a dark jewel in a gold ring, of which more anon.

Let us dwell upon the confession.   The first stage of this conscience-climax is reached by the dramatization of The Tell-tale Heart reminiscence in the memory of the dreaming man.   The episode makes a singular application of the theories with which this chapter begins.   For furniture-in-motion we have the detective's pencil.   For trappings and inventions in motion we have his tapping shoe and the busy clock pendulum.   Because this scene is so powerful the photoplay is described in this chapter rather than any other, though the application is more spiritual than literal.   The half-mad boy begins to divulge that he thinks that the habitual ticking of the clock is satanically timed to the beating of the dead man's heart.   Here more unearthliness hovers round a pendulum than any merely mechanical trick-movements could impart.   Then the merest commonplace of the detective tapping his pencil in the same time — the boy trying in vain to ignore it — increases the strain, till the audience has well-nigh the hallucinations of the victim. Then the bold tapping of the detective's foot, who would do all his accusing without saying a word, and the startling coincidence of the owl hoot-hooting outside the window to the same measure, bring us close to the final breakdown. These realistic material actors are as potent as the actual apparitions of the dead man that preceded them. Those visions prepared the mind to invest trifles with significance. The pencil and the pendulum conducting themselves in an apparently everyday fashion, satisfy in a far nobler way the thing in the cave-man attending the show that made him take note in other centuries of the rope that began to hang the butcher, the fire that began to burn the stick, and the stick that began to beat the dog.

Now the play takes a higher demoniacal plane reminiscent of Poe's Bells. The boy opens the door. He peers into the darkness. There he sees them. They are the nearest to the sinister Poe quality of any illustrations I recall that attempt it. "They are neither man nor woman, they are neither brute nor

human; they are ghouls." The scenes are designed with the architectural dignity that the
first part of this chapter has insisted wizard
trappings should take on.   Now it is that the
boy confesses and the Poe story ends.

Then comes what the photoplay people
call the punch. It is discussed at the end of
chapter nine. It is a kind of solar plexus blow
to the sensibilities, certainly by this time an
unnecessary part of the film. Usually every
soul movement carefully built up to where
the punch begins is forgotten in the material
smash or rescue. It is not so bad in this case,
but it is a too conventional proceeding for
Griffith.

The boy flees interminably to a barn too
far away.   There is a siege by a posse, led
by the detective.   It is veritable border warfare. The Italian leads an unsuccessful rescue
party. The unfortunate youth finally hangs
himself. The beautiful Annabel bursts through
the siege a moment too late; then, heart
broken, kills herself. These things are carried
out by good technicians. But it would have
been better to have had the suicide with but
a tiny part of the battle, and the story five
reels long instead of six. This physical turmoil

is carried into the spiritual world only by the psychic momentum acquired through the previous confession scene. The one thing with intrinsic pictorial heart-power is the death of Annabel by jumping off the sea cliff.

Then comes the awakening. To every one who sees the film for the first time it is like the forgiveness of sins. The boy finds his uncle still alive. In revulsion from himself, he takes the old man into his arms. The uncle has already begun to be ashamed of his terrible words, and has prayed for a contrite heart. The radiant Annabel is shown in the early dawn rising and hurrying to her lover in spite of her pride. She will bravely take back her last night's final word. She cannot live without him. The uncle makes amends to the girl. The three are in the inconsistent but very human mood of sweet forgiveness for love's sake, that sometimes overtakes the bitterest of us after some crisis in our days.

The happy pair are shown, walking through the hills. Thrown upon the clouds for them are the moods of the poet-lover's heart. They look into the woods and see his fancies of Spring, the things that he will some day write. These pageants might be longer. They furnish the great climax. They make a consistent parallel and contrast with the ghoul-visions that end with the confession to the detective. They wipe that terror from the mind. They do not represent Poe. The rabbits, the leopard, the fairies, Cupid and Psyche in the clouds, and the little loves from the hollow trees are contributions to the original poetry of the eye.

Finally, the central part of this production of the Avenging Conscience is no dilution of Poe, but an adequate interpretation, a story he might have written. Those who have the European respect for Poe's work will be most apt to be satisfied with this section, including the photographic texture which may be said to be an authentic equivalent of his prose. How often Poe has been primly patronized for his majestic quality, the wizard power which looms above all his method and subject-matter and furnishes the only reason for its existence!

For Griffith to embroider this Poe Interpretation in the centre of a fairly consistent fabric, and move on into a radiant climax of his own that is in organic relation to the whole, is an achievement indeed. The final criticism is that the play is derivative. It is not built from new material in all its parts, as

was the original story.   One must be a student
of Poe to get its ultimate flavor.   But in reading Poe's own stories, one need not be a reader
of any one special preceding writer to get the
strange and solemn exultation of that literary
enchanter.   He is the quintessence of his own
lonely soul.

Though the wizard element is paramount in
the Poe episode of this film, the appeal to the
conscience is only secondary to this.   It is
keener than in Poe, owing to the human elements before and after.   The Chameleon producer approximates in The Avenging Conscience
the type of mystic teacher, discussed in the
twentieth chapter: " The Prophet-Wizard."

CHAPTER XI

ARCHITECTURE-IN-MOTION

THIS chapter is a superstructure upon the foundations of chapters five, six, and seven.

I have said that it is a quality, not a defect, of the photoplays that while the actors tend to become types and hieroglyphics and dolls, on the other hand, dolls and hieroglyphics and mechanisms tend to become human. By an extension of this principle, non-human tones, textures, lines, and spaces take on a vitality almost like that of flesh and blood. It is partly for this reason that some energy is hereby given to the matter of reënforcing the idea that the people with the proper training to take the higher photoplays in hand are not veteran managers of vaudeville circuits, but rather painters, sculptors, and architects, preferably those who are in the flush of their first reputation in these crafts. Let us imagine the centres of the experimental drama, such as the Drama League, the Universities, and the

stage societies, calling in people of these profes-
sions and starting photoplay competitions and
enterprises.   Let the thesis be here emphasized
that the architects, above all, are the men to
advance the work in the ultra-creative photoplay. "But few architects," you say, "are
creative, even in their own profession."

Let us begin with the point of view of the
highly trained pedantic young builder, the type
that, in the past few years, has honored our
landscape with those paradoxical memorials of
Abraham Lincoln the railsplitter, memorials
whose Ionic columns are straight from Paris.
Pericles is the real hero of such a man, not
Lincoln. So let him for the time surrender
completely to that great Greek. He is worthy
of a monument nobler than any America has
set up to any one. The final pictures may be
taken in front of buildings with which the
architect or his favorite master has already
edified this republic, or if the war is over, before
some surviving old-world models. But whatever the method, let him study to express at
last the thing that moves within him as a creep-
ing fire, which Americans do not yet understand and the loss of which makes the classic
in our architecture a mere piling of elegant

stones upon one another. In the arrangement of crowds and flow of costuming and study of tableau climaxes, let the architect bring an illusion of that delicate flowering, that brilliant instant of time before the Peloponnesian war. It does not seem impossible when one remembers the achievements of the author of Cabiria in approximating Rome and Carthage.

Let the principal figure of the pageant be the virgin Athena, walking as a presence visible only to us, yet among her own people, and robed and armed and panoplied, the guardian of Pericles, appearing in those streets that were herself. Let the architect show her as she came only in a vision to Phidias, while the dramatic writers and mathematicians and poets and philosophers go by. The crowds should be like pillars of Athens, and she like a great pillar. The crowds should be like the tossing waves of the Ionic Sea and Athena like the white ship upon the waves. The audiences in the tragedies should be shown like wheat-fields on the hill-sides, always stately yet blown by the wind, and Athena the one sower and reaper. Crowds should descend the steps of the Acropolis, nymphs and fauns and

Olympians, carved as it were from the marble, yet flowing like a white cataract down into the town, bearing with them Athena, their soul. All this in the Photoplay of Pericles.

No civic or national incarnation since that time appeals to the poets like the French worship of the Maid of Orleans. In Percy MacKaye's book, The Present Hour, he says on the French attitude toward the war : —

"Half artist and half anchorite,
  Part siren and part Socrates,
  Her face — alluring fair, yet recondite —
  Smiled through her salons and academies.

  Lightly she wore her double mask,
  Till sudden, at war's kindling spark,
  Her inmost self, in shining mail and casque,
  Blazed to the world her single soul — Jeanne
    d' Arc!"

To make a more elaborate showing of what is meant by architecture-in-motion, let us progress through the centuries and suppose that the builder has this enthusiasm for France, that he is slowly setting about to build a photoplay around the idea of the Maid.

First let him take the mural painting point of

view.   Bear in mind these characteristics of that
art : it is wall-painting that is an organic part
of the surface on which it appears : it is on
the same lines as the building and adapted to
the colors and forms of the structure of which
it is a part.

The wall-splendors of America that are the
most scattered about in inexpensive copies
are the decorations of the Boston Public
Library.   Note the pillar-like quality of Sar-
gent's prophets, the solemn dignity of Abbey's
Holy Grail series, the grand horizontals and
perpendiculars of the work of Puvis de Cha-
vannes.   The last is the orthodox mural painter
of the world, but the other two will serve the
present   purpose   also.   These architectural
paintings if they were dramatized, still retaining their powerful lines, would be three exceedingly varied examples of what is meant by
architecture-in-motion.   The visions that appear to Jeanne d'Arc might be delineated in the
mood of some one of these three painters.   The
styles will not mix in the same episode.

A painter from old time we mention here,
not because he was orthodox, but because of
his genius for the drawing of action, and because he covered tremendous wall-spaces with

Venetian tone and color, is Tintoretto.   If there
is a mistrust that the mural painting standard
will tend to destroy the sense of action, Tintoretto will restore confidence in that regard.
As the Winged Victory represents flying in
sculpture, so his work is the extreme example
of action with the brush.   The Venetians called
him the furious painter.   One must understand
a man through his admirers.   So explore
Ruskin's sayings on Tintoretto.

I have a dozen moving picture magazine
clippings, which are in their humble way first
or second cousins of mural paintings.   I will describe but two, since the method of selection has
already been amply indicated, and the reader
can find his own examples.   For a Crowd Picture, for instance, here is a scene at a masquerade ball.   The glitter of the costumes is
an extension of the glitter of the candelabra
overhead.   The people are as it were chande-
liers, hung lower down.   The lines of the
candelabra relate to the very ribbon streamers
of the heroine, and the massive wood-work is
the big brother of the square-shouldered heroes
in the foreground, though one is a clown, one
is a Russian Duke, and one is Don Cæsar
De Bazan.   The building is the father of the

people. These relations can be kept in the court scenes of the production of Jeanne d'Arc.

Here is a night picture from a war story in which the light is furnished by two fires whose coals and brands are hidden by earth heaped in front. The sentiment of tenting on the old camp-ground pervades the scene. The far end of the line of those keeping bivouac disappears into the distance, and the depths of the ranks behind them fade into the thick shadows. The flag, a little above the line, catches the light. One great tree overhead spreads its leafless half-lit arms through the gloom. Behind all this is unmitigated black. The composition reminds one of a Hiroshige study of midnight. These men are certainly a part of the architecture of out of doors, and mysterious as the vault of Heaven. This type of a camp-fire is possible in our Jeanne d'Arc.

These pictures, new and old, great and unknown, indicate some of the standards of judgment and types of vision whereby our conception of the play is to be evolved.

By what means shall we block it in? Our friend Tintoretto made use of methods which are here described from one of his biographers,

W. Roscoe Osler: "They have been much enlarged upon in the different biographies as
the means whereby Tintoretto obtained his
power. They constituted, however, his habitual method of determining the effect and general grouping of his compositions. He moulded
with extreme care small models of his figures
in wax and clay. Titian and other painters
as well as Tintoretto employed this method
as the means of determining the light and
shade of their design. Afterwards the later
stages of their work were painted from the
life. But in Tintoretto's compositions the
position and arrangement of his figures as he
began to dwell upon his great conceptions
were such as to render the study from the living model a matter of great difficulty and at
times an impossibility. . . . He . . . modelled his sculptures . . . imparting to his
models a far more complete character than had
been customary. These firmly moulded figures,
sometimes draped, sometimes free, he sus-
pended in a box made of wood, or of cardboard
for his smaller work, in whose walls he made
an aperture to admit a lighted candle. . . .
He sits moving the light about amidst his
assemblage of figures. Every aspect of sublim-

ity of light suitable to a Madonna surrounded
with angels, or a heavenly choir, finds its minia-
ture response among the figures as the light
moves.

" This was the method by which, in con-
junction with a profound study of outward
nature, sympathy with the beauty of different
types of face and varieties of form, with the
many changing hues of the Venetian scene,
with the great laws of color and a knowledge
of literature and history, he was able to shadow
forth his great imagery of the intuitional
world."

This method of Tintoretto suggests several
possible derivatives in the preparation of motion
pictures.   Let the painters and sculptors be now
called upon for painting models and sculptural
models, while the architect, already present,
supplies the architectural models, all three
giving us visible scenarios to furnish the cardinal motives for the acting, from which the
amateur photoplay company of the university
can begin their interpretation.

For episodes that follow the precedent of the
simple Action Film tiny wax models of the
figures, toned and costumed to the heart's
delight, would tell the high points of the story.

Let them represent, perhaps, seven crucial situations from the proposed photoplay. Let them be designed as uniquely in their dresses as are the Russian dancers' dresses, by Léon Bakst. Then to alternate with these, seven little paintings of episodes, designed in blacks, whites, and grays, each representing some elusive point in the intimate aspects of the story. Let there be a definite system of space and texture relations retained throughout the set.

The models for the splendor scenes would, of course, be designed by the architect, and these other scenes alternated with and subordinated to his work. The effects which he would conceive would be on a grander scale. The models for these might be mere extensions of the methods of those others, but in the typical and highest let us imagine ourselves going beyond Tintoretto in preparation.

Let the principal splendor moods and effects be indicated by actual structures, such miniatures as architects offer along with their plans of public buildings, but transfigured beyond that standard by the light of inspiration combined with experimental candle-light, spotlight, sunlight, or torchlight. They must not be conceived as stage arrangements of wax

figures with harmonious and fitting backgrounds, but as backgrounds that clamor for
utterance through the figures in front of them,
as Athens finds her soul in the Athena with
which we began. These three sorts of models,
properly harmonized, should have with them
a written scenario constructed to indicate
all the scenes between. The scenario will lead
up to these models for climaxes and hold them
together in the celestial hurdle-race.

We have in our museums some definite architectural suggestions as to the style of these
models. There are in Blackstone Hall in the
Chicago Art Institute several great Romanesque
and Gothic portals, pillars, and statues that
might tell directly upon certain settings of our
Jeanne d'Arc pageant. They are from Notre
Dame du Port at Clermont-Ferrand, the Abbey
church of St. Gilles, the Abbey of Charlieu,
the Cathedral of Amiens, Notre Dame at
Paris, the Cathedral of Bordeaux, and the
Cathedral of Rheims. Perhaps the object I
care for most in the Metropolitan Museum,
New York, is the complete model of Notre
Dame, Paris, by M. Joly. Why was this model
of Notre Dame made with such exquisite
pains? Certainly not as a matter of mere

information or cultivation. I venture the first right these things have to be taken care of in museums is to stimulate to new creative effort.

I went to look over the Chicago collection with a friend and poet Arthur Davison Ficke. He said something to this effect: "The first thing I see when I look at these fragments is the whole cathedral in all its original proportions. Then I behold the mediæval marketplace hunched against the building, burying the foundations, the life of man growing rank and weedlike around it. Then I see the bishop coming from the door with his impressive train. But a crusade may go by on the way to the Holy Land. A crusade may come home battered and in rags. I get the sense of life, as of a rapid in a river flowing round a great rock."

The cathedral stands for the age-long meditation of the ascetics in the midst of battling tribes. This brooding architecture has a blood-brotherhood with the meditating, saint-seeing Jeanne d'Arc.

There is in the Metropolitan Museum a large and famous canvas painted by the dying Bastien-Lepage; — Jeanne Listening to the Voices. It is a picture of which the technicians and the

poets are equally enamored.   The tale of Jeanne
d'Arc could be told, carrying this particular
peasant girl through the story.   And for a
piece of architectural pageantry akin to the
photoplay ballroom scene already described,
yet far above it, there is nothing more apt for
our purpose than the painting by Boutet de
Monvel filling the space at the top of the stair
at the Chicago Art Institute.   Though the
Bastien-Lepage is a large painting, this is
many times the size.   It shows Joan's visit
at the court of Chinon.   It is big without
being empty.   It conveys a glitter which expresses one of the things that is meant by the
phrase: Splendor Photoplay.   But for moving
picture purposes it is the Bastien-Lepage Joan
that should appear here, set in dramatic contrast to the Boutet de Monvel Court.   Two
valuable neighbors to whom I have read this
chapter suggest that the whole Boutet de
Monvel illustrated child's book about our
heroine could be used on this grand scale, for
a background.

The Inness room at the Chicago Art Institute
is another school for the meditative producer,
if he would evolve his tribute to France on
American soil.   Though no photoplay tableau

has yet approximated the brush of Inness, why not attempt to lead Jeanne through an Inness landscape? The Bastien-Lepage trees are in France. But here is an American world in which one could see visions and hear voices. Where is the inspired camera that will record something of what Inness beheld?

Thus much for the atmosphere and trappings of our Jeanne d'Arc scenario. Where will we get our story? It should, of course, be written from the ground up for this production, but as good Americans we would probably find a mass of suggestions in Mark Twain's Joan of Arc.

Quite recently a moving picture company sent its photographers to Springfield, Illinois, and produced a story with our city for a background, using our social set for actors. Backed by the local commercial association for whose benefit the thing was made, the resources of the place were at the command of routine producers. Springfield dressed its best, and acted with fair skill. The heroine was a charming débutante, the hero the son of Governor Dunne. The Mine Owner's Daughter was at best a mediocre photoplay. But this type of social-artistic event, that happened once, may be attempted a hundred times, each time slowly improving. Which brings us to something that is in the end very far from The Mine Owner's Daughter. By what scenario method the following film or series of films is to be produced I will not venture to say. No doubt the way will come if once the dream has a sufficient hold.

I have long maintained that my home-town should have a goddess like Athena. The legend should be forthcoming. The producer, while not employing armies, should use many actors and the tale be told with the same power with which the productions of Judith of Bethulia and The Battle Hymn of the Republic were evolved. While the following story may not be the form which Springfield civic religion will ultimately take, it is here recorded as a second cousin of the dream that I hope will some day be set forth.

Late in an afternoon in October, a light is seen in the zenith like a dancing star. The clouds form round it in the approximation of a circle. Now there becomes visible a group of heads and shoulders of presences that are looking down through the ring of clouds, watching the star, like giant children that peep down a well. The jewel descends by four sparkling chains, so far away they look to be dewy threads of silk. As the bright mystery grows larger it appears to be approaching the treeless hill of Washington Park, a hill that is surrounded by many wooded ridges. The people come running from everywhere to watch. Here indeed will be a Crowd Picture with as many phases as a stormy ocean. Flying machines appear from the Fair Ground north of the city, and circle round and round as they go up, trying to reach the slowly descending plummet.

At last, while the throng cheers, one bird-man has attained it. He brings back his message that the gift is an image, covered loosely with a wrapping that seems to be of spun gold. Now the many aviators whirl round the descending wonder, like seagulls playing about a ship's mast. Soon, amid an awestruck throng, the image is on the hillock. The golden chains, and the giant children holding them there above, have melted into threads of mist and nothingness. The shining wrapping falls away. The people look upon a seated statue of marble and gold. There is a branch of wrought-gold maple leaves in her hands. Then beside the image is a fluttering transfigured presence of which the image seems to be a representation. This spirit, carrying a living maple branch in her hand, says to the people: "Men and Women of Springfield, this carving is the Lady Springfield sent by your Lord from Heaven. Build no canopy over her. Let her ever be under the prairie-sky. Do her perpetual honor." The messenger, who is the soul and voice of Springfield, fades into the crowd, to emerge on great and terrible occasions.

This is only one story. Round this public event let the photoplay romancer weave what tales of private fortune he will, narratives bound up with the events of that October day, as the story of Nathan and Naomi is woven into Judith of Bethulia.

Henceforth the city officers are secular priests of Our Lady Springfield. Their failure in duty is a profanation of her name. A yearly pledge of the first voters is taken in her presence like the old Athenian oath of citizenship. The seasonal pageants march to the statue's feet, scattering flowers. The important outdoor festivals are given on the edge of her hill. All the roads lead to her footstool. Pilgrims come from the Seven Seas to look upon her face that is carved by Invisible Powers. Moreover, the living messenger that is her actual soul appears in dreams, or visions of the open day, when the days are dark for the city, when her patriots are irresolute, and her children are put to shame.   This spirit with the maple branch rallies them, leads them to victories like those that were won of old in the **name of Jeanne d'Arc or Pallas Athena herself.**

CHAPTER XII

THE stage is dependent upon three lines of tradition: first, that of Greece and Rome that came down through the French. Second, the English style, ripened from the miracle play and the Shakespearian stage. And third, the Ibsen precedent from Norway, now so firmly established it is classic. These methods are obscured by the commercialized dramas, but they are behind them all. Let us discuss for illustration the Ibsen tradition.

Ibsen is generally the vitriolic foe of pageant. He must be read aloud. He stands for the spoken word, for the iron power of life that may be concentrated in a phrase like the "All or nothing" of Brand. Though Peer Gynt has its spectacular side, Ibsen generally comes in through the ear alone. He can be acted in essentials from end to end with one table and four chairs in any parlor. The alleged punch with which the "movie" culminates has occurred

three or ten years before the Ibsen curtain goes
up.   At the close of every act of the dramas of
this Norwegian one might inscribe on the curtain
"This the magnificent moving picture cannot
achieve."   Likewise after every successful film
described in this book could be inscribed "This
the trenchant Ibsen cannot do."

But a photoplay of Ghosts came to our town.
The humor of the prospect was the sort too
deep for tears.   My pastor and I reread the
William Archer translation that we might be
alert for every antithesis.   Together we went
to the services.   Since then the film has been
furiously denounced by the literati.   Floyd
Dell's discriminating assault upon it is quoted
in Current Opinion, October, 1915, and Margaret
Anderson prints a denunciation of it in a recent
number of The Little Review.   But it is not
such a bad film in itself.   It is not Ibsen.   It
should be advertised "The Iniquities of the
Fathers, an American drama of Eugenics, in a
Palatial Setting."

Henry Walthall as Alving, afterward as his
son, shows the men much as Ibsen outlines
their characters.   Of course the only way to be
Ibsen is to be so precisely.   In the new plot all
is open as the day.   The world is welcome, and

generally present when the man or his son go
forth to see the elephant and hear the owl.
Provincial hypocrisy is not implied. But
Ibsen can scarcely exist without an atmosphere
of secrecy for his human volcanoes to burst
through in the end.

Mary Alden as Mrs. Alving shows in her
intelligent and sensitive countenance that she
has a conception of that character. She does
not always have the chance to act the woman
written in her face, the tart, thinking, handsome
creature that Ibsen prefers. Nigel Debrullier
looks the buttoned-up Pastor Manders, even to
caricature. But the crawling, bootlicking car-
penter, Jacob Engstrand, is changed into a respectable, guileless man with an income. And
his wife and daughter are helpless, conventional,
upper-class rabbits. They do not remind one
of the saucy originals.

The original Ibsen drama is the result of
mixing up five particular characters through
three acts. There is not a situation but
would go to pieces if one personality were
altered. Here are two, sadly tampered with:
Engstrand and his daughter. Here is the
mother, who is only referred to in Ibsen.
Here is the elder Alving, who disappears be-

fore the original play starts. So the twenty great Ibsen situations in the stage production are gone. One new crisis has an Ibsen irony and psychic tension. The boy is taken with the dreaded intermittent pains in the back of his head. He is painting the order that is to make him famous : the King's portrait. While the room empties of people he writhes on the floor. If this were all, it would have been one more moving picture failure to put through a tragic scene. But the thing is reiterated in tableau-symbol. He is looking sideways in terror. A hairy arm with clutching demon claws comes thrusting in toward the back of his neck. He writhes in deadly fear. The audience is appalled for him.

This visible clutch of heredity is the nearest equivalent that is offered for the whispered refrain : " Ghosts," in the original masterpiece. This hand should also be reiterated as a re-frain, three times at least, before this tableau, each time more dreadful and threatening. It appears but the once, and has no chance to become a part of the accepted hieroglyphics of the piece, as it should be, to realize its full power.

The father's previous sins have been acted out.

The boy's consequent struggle with the malady has been traced step by step, so the play should end here. It would then be a rough equivalent of the Ibsen irony in a contrary medium. Instead of that, it wanders on through paraphrases of scraps of the play, sometimes literal, then quite alien, on to the alleged motion picture punch, when the Doctor is the god from the machine. There is no doctor on the stage in the original Ghosts. But there is a physician in the Doll's House, a scientific, quietly moving oracle, crisp, Spartan, sophisticated.

Is this photoplay physician such a one? The boy and his half-sister are in their wedding-clothes in the big church. Pastor Manders is saying the ceremony. The audience and building are indeed showy. The doctor charges up the aisle at the moment people are told to speak or forever hold their peace. He has tact. He simply breaks up the marriage right there. He does not tell the guests why. But he takes the wedding party into the pastor's study and there blazes at the bride and groom the long-suppressed truth that they are brother and sister. Always an orotund man, he has the Chautauqua manner indeed in this exigency.

He brings to one's mind the tearful book, much loved in childhood, Parted at the Altar, or Why Was it Thus? And four able actors have the task of telling the audience by facial expression only, that they have been struck by moral lightning. They stand in a row, facing the people, endeavoring to make the crisis of an alleged Ibsen play out of a crashing melodrama.

The final death of young Alving is depicted with an approximation of Ibsen's mood. But the only ways to suggest such feelings in silence, do not convey them in full to the audience, but merely narrate them. Wherever in Ghosts we have quiet voices that are like the slow drip of hydrochloric acid, in the photoplay we have no quiet gestures that will do trenchant work. Instead there are endless writhings and rushings about, done with a deal of skill, but destructive of the last remnants of Ibsen.

Up past the point of the clutching hand this film is the prime example for study for the person who would know once for all the differences between the photoplays and the stage dramas. Along with it might be classed Mrs. Fiske's decorative moving picture Tess, in which there is every determination to convey the original Mrs. Fiske illusion without her voice and breathing presence. To people who know her well it is a surprisingly good tintype of our beloved friend, for the family album. The relentless Thomas Hardy is nowhere to be found. There are two moments of dramatic life set among many of delicious pictorial quality: when Tess baptizes her child, and when she smooths its little grave with a wavering hand. But in the stage-version the dramatic poignancy begins with the going up of the curtain, and lasts till it descends.

The prime example of complete failure is Sarah Bernhardt's Camille. It is indeed a tintype of the consumptive heroine, with every group entire, and taken at full length. Much space is occupied by the floor and the overhead portions of the stage setting. It lasts as long as would the spoken performance, and wherever there is a dialogue we must imagine said conversation if we can. It might be compared to watching Camille from the top gallery through smoked glass, with one's ears stopped with cotton.

It would be well for the beginning student to find some way to see the first two of these three, or some other attempts to revamp the

classic, for instance Mrs. Fiske's painstaking
reproduction of Vanity Fair, bearing in mind
the list of differences which this chapter now
furnishes.

There is no denying that many stage managers who have taken up photoplays are strug-
gling with the Shakespearian French and Norwegian traditions in the new medium. Many
of the moving pictures discussed in this book
are rewritten stage dramas, and one, Judith
of Bethulia, is a pronounced success. But in
order to be real photoplays the stage dramas
must be overhauled indeed, turned inside out
and upside down. The successful motion picture expresses itself through mechanical devices
that are being evolved every hour. Upon
those many new bits of machinery are founded
novel methods of combination in another field
of logic, not dramatic logic, but tableau logic.
But the old-line managers, taking up photoplays,
begin by making curious miniatures of stage
presentations. They try to have most things as
before. Later they take on the moving picture
technique in a superficial way, but they, and
the host of talented actors in the prime of life
and Broadway success, retain the dramatic
state of mind.

It is a principle of criticism, the world over, that the distinctions between the arts must be clearly marked, even by those who afterwards mix those arts. Take, for instance, the perpetual quarrel between the artists and the half-educated about literary painting. Whistler fought that battle in England. He tried to beat it into the head of John Bull that a painting is one thing, a mere illustration for a story another thing. But the novice is always stubborn. To him Hindu and Arabic are both foreign languages, therefore just alike. The book illustration may be said to come in through the ear, by reading the title aloud in imagination. And the other is effective with no title at all. The scenario writer who will study to the bottom of the matter in Whistler's Gentle Art of Making Enemies will be equipped to welcome the distinction between the old-fashioned stage, where the word rules, and the photoplay, where splendor and ritual are all. It is not the same distinction, but a kindred one.

But let us consider the details of the matter. The stage has its exits and entrances at the side and back. The standard photoplays have their exits and entrances across the imaginary

footlight line, even in the most stirring mob
and battle scenes. In Judith of Bethulia,
though the people seem to be coming from
everywhere and going everywhere, when we
watch close, we see that the individuals enter
at the near right-hand corner and exit at the
near left-hand corner, or enter at the near
left-hand corner and exit at the near right-
hand corner.

Consider the devices whereby the stage actor
holds the audience as he goes out at the side
and back. He sighs, gestures, howls, and strides.
With what studious preparation he ripens his
quietness, if he goes out that way. In the
new contraption, the moving picture, the hero
or villain in exit strides past the nose of the
camera, growing much bigger than a human
being, marching toward us as though he would
step on our heads, disappearing when largest.
There is an explosive power about the mildest
motion picture exit, be the actor skilful or
the reverse. The people left in the scene are
pygmies compared with each disappearing
cyclops. Likewise, when the actor enters again,
his mechanical importance is overwhelming.
Therefore, for his first entrance the motion
picture star does not require the preparations

that are made on the stage. The support does not need to warm the spectators to the problem, then talk them into surrender.

When the veteran stage-producer as a beginning photoplay producer tries to give us a dialogue in the motion pictures, he makes it so dull no one follows. He does not realize that his camera-born opportunity to magnify persons and things instantly, to interweave them as actors on one level, to alternate scenes at the slightest whim, are the big substitutes for dialogue. By alternating scenes rapidly, flash after flash: cottage, field, mountain-top, field, mountain-top, cottage, we have a conversation between three places rather than three persons. By alternating the picture of a man and the check he is forging, we have his soliloquy. When two people talk to each other, it is by lifting and lowering objects rather than their voices. The collector presents a bill: the adventurer shows him the door. The boy plucks a rose: the girl accepts it. Moving objects, not moving lips, make the words of the photoplay.

The old-fashioned stage producer, feeling he is getting nowhere, but still helpless, puts the climax of some puzzling lip-debate, often the climax of the whole film, as a sentence on the screen. Sentences should be used to show changes of time and place and a few such elementary matters before the episode is fully started. The climax of a motion picture scene cannot be one word or fifty words. As has been discussed in connection with Cabiria, the crisis must be an action sharper than any that has gone before in organic union with a tableau more beautiful than any that has preceded: the breaking of the tenth wave upon the sand. Such remnants of pantomimic dialogue as remain in the main chase of the photoplay film are but guide-posts in the race toward the goal. They should not be elaborate toll-gates of plot, to be laboriously lifted and lowered while the horses stop, mid-career.

The Venus of Milo, that comes directly to the soul through the silence, requires no quotation from Keats to explain her, though Keats is the equivalent in verse. Her setting in the great French Museum is enough. We do not know that her name is Venus. She is thought by many to be another statue of Victory. We may some day evolve scenarios that will require nothing more than a title thrown upon the screen at the beginning, they come to the eye so perfectly. This is not the only possible

sort, but the self-imposed limitation in certain
films might give them a charm akin to that of
the Songs without Words.

The stage audience is a unit of three hundred
or a thousand. In the beginning of the first
act there is much moving about and extra
talk on the part of the actors, to hold the crowd
while it is settling down, and enable the late-
comer to be in his seat before the vital part
of the story starts. If he appears later, he
is glared at. In the motion picture art gallery,
on the other hand, the audience is around two
hundred, and these are not a unit, and the only
crime is to obstruct the line of vision. The
high-school girls can do a moderate amount of
giggling without breaking the spell. There is
no spell, in the stage sense, to break. People
can climb over each other's knees to get in or
out. If the picture is political, they murmur
war-cries to one another. If the film suggests
what some of the neighbors have been doing,
they can regale each other with the richest
sewing society report.

The people in the motion picture audience
total about two hundred, any time, but they
come in groups of two or three at no specified
hour. The newcomers do not, as in Vaudeville,

make themselves part of a jocular army. Strictly as individuals they judge the panorama. If they disapprove, there is grumbling under their breath, but no hissing. I have never heard an audience in a photoplay theatre clap its hands even when the house was bursting with people. Yet they often see the film through twice. When they have had enough, they stroll home. They manifest their favorable verdict by sending some other member of the family to "see the picture." If the people so delegated are likewise satisfied, they may ask the man at the door if he is going to bring it back. That is the moving picture kind of cheering.

It was a theatrical sin when the old-fashioned stage actor was rendered unimportant by his scenery. But the motion picture actor is but the mood of the mob or the landscape or the department store behind him, reduced to a single hieroglyphic.

The stage-interior is large. The motion-picture interior is small. The stage out-of-door scene is at best artificial and little and is generally at rest, or its movement is tainted with artificiality. The waves dash, but not dashingly, the water flows, but not flowingly.

The motion picture out-of-door scene is as big as the universe. And only pictures of the Sahara are without magnificent motion.

The photoplay is as far from the stage on the one hand as it is from the novel on the other. Its nearest analogy in literature is, perhaps, the short story, or the lyric poem. The key-words of the stage are *passion* and *character;* of the photoplay, *splendor* and *speed.* The stage in its greatest power deals with pity for some one especially unfortunate, with whom we grow well acquainted; with some private revenge against some particular despoiler; traces the beginning and culmination of joy based on the gratification of some preference, or love for some person, whose charm is all his own. The drama is concerned with the slow, inevitable approaches to these intensities. On the other hand, the motion picture, though often appearing to deal with these things, as a matter of fact uses substitutes, many of which have been listed. But to review: its first substitute is the excitement of speed-mania stretched on the framework of an obvious plot. Or it deals with delicate informal anecdote as the short story does, or fairy legerdemain, or patriotic banners, or great surging mobs of the proletariat, or big scenic

outlooks, or miraculous beings made visible.
And the further it gets from Euripides, Ibsen,
Shakespeare, or Molière — the more it becomes
like a mural painting from which flashes of
lightning come — the more it realizes its genius.
Men like Gordon Craig and Granville Barker
are almost wasting their genius on the theatre.
The Splendor Photoplays are the great outlet
for their type of imagination.

The typical stage performance is from two
hours and a half upward. The movie show
generally lasts five reels, that is, an hour and
forty minutes. And it should last but three
reels, that is, an hour. Edgar Poe said there
was no such thing as a long poem. There is
certainly no such thing as a long moving picture masterpiece.

The stage-production depends most largely
upon the power of the actors, the movie show
upon the genius of the producer. The performers and the dumb objects are on equal
terms in his paint-buckets. The star-system is
bad for the stage because the minor parts are
smothered and the situations distorted to give
the favorite an orbit. It is bad for the motion
pictures because it obscures the producer.
While the leading actor is entitled to his glory,

as are all the actors, their mannerisms should
not overshadow the latest inspirations of the
creator of the films.

The display of the name of the corporation
is no substitute for giving the glory to the producer. An artistic photoplay is not the result
of a military efficiency system. It is not a
factory-made staple article, but the product of
the creative force of one soul, the flowering of
a spirit that has the habit of perpetually renewing itself.

Once I saw Mary Fuller in a classic. It was
the life and death of Mary Queen of Scots.
Not only was the tense, fidgety, over-American
Mary Fuller transformed into a being who was
a poppy and a tiger-lily and a snow-queen and
a rose, but she and her company, including
Marc Macdermott, radiated the old Scotch
patriotism. They made the picture a memorial.
It reminded one of Maurice Hewlett's novel
The Queen's Quair. Evidently all the actors
were fused by some noble managerial mood.

There can be no doubt that so able a group
have evolved many good films that have escaped
me. But though I did go again and again,
never did I see them act with the same deliberation and distinction, and I laid the difference

to a change in the state of mind of the producer.   Even baseball players must have managers.   A team cannot pick itself, or it surely
would.   And this rule may apply to the stage.
But by comparison to motion picture performers, stage-actors are their own managers,
for they have an approximate notion of how
they look in the eye of the audience, which is
but the human eye.   They can hear and gauge
their own voices.   They have the same ears as
their listeners.   But the picture producer holds
to his eyes the seven-leagued demon spy-glass
called the kinetoscope, as the audience will do
later.   The actors have not the least notion
of their appearance.   Also the words in the
motion picture are not things whose force the
actor can gauge.   The book under the table is
one word, the dog behind the chair is another,
the window curtain flying in the breeze is
another.

This chapter has implied that the performers were but paint on the canvas.   They
are both paint and models.   They are models
in the sense that the young Ellen Terry was
the inspiration for Watts' Sir Galahad.   They
resemble the persons in private life who furnish
the basis for novels.   Dickens' mother was the

original of Mrs. Nickleby. His father entered into Wilkins Micawber. But these people are not perpetually thrust upon us as Mr. and Mrs. Dickens. We are glad to find them in the Dickens biographies. When the stories begin, it is Micawber and Mrs. Nickleby we want, and the Charles Dickens atmosphere.

The photoplays of the future will be written from the foundations for the films. The soundest actors, photographers, and producers will be those who emphasize the points wherein the photoplay is unique. What is adapted to complete expression in one art generally secures but half expression in another. The supreme photoplay will give us things that have been but half expressed in all other mediums allied to it.

Once this principle is grasped there is every reason why the same people who have interested themselves in the advanced experimental drama should take hold of the super-photoplay. The good citizens who can most easily grasp the distinction should be there to perpetuate the higher welfare of these institutions side by side. This parallel development should come, if for no other reason, because the two arts are still roughly classed together by the public. The elect cannot teach the public what the drama is till they show them precisely what the photoplay is and is not. Just as the university has departments of both History and English teaching in amity, each one illuminating the work of the other, so these two forms should live in each other's sight in fine and friendly contrast. At present they are in blind and jealous warfare.

CHAPTER XIII

HIEROGLYPHICS

I HAVE read this chapter to a pretty neighbor who has approved of the preceding portions of the book, whose mind, therefore, I cannot but respect. My neighbor classes this discussion of hieroglyphics as a fanciful flight rather than a sober argument. I submit the verdict, then struggle against it while you read.

The invention of the photoplay is as great a step as was the beginning of picture-writing in the stone age. And the cave-men and women of our slums seem to be the people most affected by this novelty, which is but an expression of the old in that spiral of life which is going higher while seeming to repeat the ancient phase.

There happens to be here on the table a book on Egypt by Rawlinson that I used to thumb long ago. A footnote says: "The font of hieroglyphic type used in this work contains eight hundred forms. But there are many other forms beside." There is more light on Egypt in later works than in Rawlinson, but the statement quoted will serve for our text.

Several complex methods of making visible scenarios are listed in this work. Here is one that is mechanically simple. Let the man searching for tableau combinations, even if he is of the practical commercial type, prepare himself with eight hundred signs from Egypt. He can construct the outlines of his scenarios by placing these little pictures in rows. It may not be impractical to cut his hundreds of them from black cardboard and shuffle them on his table every morning. The list will contain all elementary and familiar things. Let him first give the most literal meaning to the patterns. Then if he desires to rise above the commercial field, let him turn over each cardboard, making the white undersurface uppermost, and there write a more abstract meaning of the hieroglyphic, one that has a fairly close relation to his way of thinking about the primary form. From a proper balance of primary and secondary meanings photoplays with souls could come. Not that he must needs become an expert Egyptologist. Yet it would profit any photoplay man to study to think like the Egyptians,

the great picture-writing people. There is as
much reason for this course as for the Bible
student's apprenticeship in Hebrew.

Hieroglyphics can prove their worth, even
without the help of an Egyptian history.
Humorous and startling analogies can be
pointed out by opening the Standard Dictionary, page fifty-nine. Look under the word
alphabet. There is the diagram of the evolution of inscriptions from the Egyptian and
Phœnician idea of what letters should be, on
through the Greek and Roman systems.

In the Egyptian row is the picture of a
throne, that has its equivalent in the Roman
letter C. And a throne has as much place in
what might be called the moving-picture
alphabet as the letter C has in ours. There
are sometimes three thrones in this small town
of Springfield in an evening. When you see
one flashed on the screen, you know instantly
you are dealing with royalty or its implications.
The last one I saw that made any particular impression was when Mary Pickford acted in Such
a Little Queen. I only wished then that she had
a more convincing throne. Let us cut one out
of black cardboard. Turning the cardboard
over to write on it the spirit-meaning, we in-

scribe some such phrase as The Throne of
Wisdom or The Throne of Liberty.

Here is the hieroglyphic of a hand:
Roman equivalent, the letter D. The human
hand, magnified till it is as big as the whole
screen, is as useful in the moving picture alphabet as the letter D in the printed alphabet.
This hand may open a lock. It may pour
poison in a bottle. It may work a telegraph
key. Then turning the white side of the cardboard uppermost we inscribe something to the
effect that this hand may write on the wall,
as at the feast of Belshazzar. Or it may represent some such conception as Rodin's Hand
of God, discussed in the Sculpture-in-motion
chapter.

Here is a duck: Roman equivalent, the
letter Z. In the motion pictures this bird,
a somewhat z-shaped animal, suggests the
finality of Arcadian peace. It is the last
and fittest ornament of the mill-pond. Nothing very terrible can happen with a duck in the
foreground. There is no use turning it over.
It would take Maeterlinck or Swedenborg to
find the mystic meaning of a duck. A duck
looks to me like a caricature of an alder-
man.

Here is a sieve: ● Roman equivalent, H. A sieve placed on the kitchen-table, close-up, suggests domesticity, hired girl humors, broad farce. We will expect the bride to make her first cake, or the flour to begin to fly into the face of the intrusive ice-man. But, as to the other side of the cardboard, the sieve has its place in higher symbolism. It has been recorded by many a sage and singer that the Almighty Powers sift men like wheat.

Here is the picture of a bowl: ◖◗ Roman equivalent, the letter K. A bowl seen through the photoplay window on the cottage table suggests Johnny's early supper of bread and milk. But as to the white side of the cardboard, out of a bowl of kindred form Omar may take his moonlit wine, or the higher gods may lift up the very wine of time to the lips of men, as Swinburne sings in Atalanta in Calydon.

Here is a lioness: ◣ Roman equivalent, the letter L. The lion or lioness creeps through the photoplay jungle to give the primary picture-word of terror in this new universal alphabet. The present writer has seen several valuable lions unmistakably shot and killed in the motion pictures, and charged up to profit and loss, just as steam-engines or houses are sometimes blown up or burned down. But of late there is a disposition to use the trained lion (or lioness) for all sorts of effects. No doubt the king and queen of beasts will become as versatile and humbly useful as the letter L itself: that is, in the commonplace routine photoplay. We turn the cardboard over and the lion becomes a resource of glory and terror, a symbol of cruel persecutions or death-less courage, sign of the zodiac that Poe in Ulalume calls the Lair of the Lion.

Here is an owl: ⚫ Roman equivalent, the letter M. The only use of the owl I can record is to be inscribed on the white surface. In The Avenging Conscience, as described in chapter ten, the murderer marks the ticking of the heart of his victim while watching the swinging of the pendulum of the old clock, then in watching the tapping of the detective's pencil on the table, then in the tapping of his foot on the floor. Finally a handsome owl is shown in the branches outside hoot-hooting in time with the action of the pencil, and the pendulum, and the dead man's heart.

But here is a wonderful thing, an actual pic-ture that has lived on, retaining its ancient imitative sound and form : ∿∿∿∿ the letter N, the drawing of a wave, with the sound of a wave still within it.   One could well imagine the Nile in the winds of the dawn making such a sound : "NN, N, N," lapping at the reeds upon its banks.   Certainly the glittering water scenes are a dominant part of moving picture Esperanto.   On the white reverse of the symbol, the spiritual meaning of water will range from the metaphor of the purity of the dew to the sea as a sign of infinity.

Here is a window with closed shutters : Latin equivalent, the letter **P**.   It is a reminder of the technical outline of this book.   The Intimate Photoplay, as I have said, is but a window where we open the shutters and peep into some one's cottage.   As to the soul meaning in the opening or closing of the shutters, it ranges from Noah's opening the hatches to send forth the dove, to the promises of blessing when the Windows of Heaven should be opened.

Here is the picture of an angle : Latin equivalent, **Q**.   This is another reminder of the technical outline.   The photoplay interior, as has been reiterated, is small and three-cornered.

Here the heroine does her plotting, flirting, and primping, etc. I will leave the spiritual interpretation of the angle to Emerson, Swedenborg, or Maeterlinck.

Here is the picture of a mouth : ◀━━▶ Latin equivalent, the letter R. If we turn from the dictionary to the monuments, we will see that the Egyptians used all the human features in their pictures. We do not separate the features as frequently as did that ancient people, but we conventionalize them as often. Nine-tenths of the actors have faces as fixed as the masks of the Greek chorus : they have the hero-mask with the protruding chin, the villain-frown, the comedian-grin, the fixed innocent-girl simper. These formulas have their place in the broad effects of Crowd Pictures and in comedies. Then there are sudden abandonments of the mask. Griffith's pupils, Henry Walthall and Blanche Sweet, seem to me to be the greatest people in the photoplays : for one reason their faces are as sensitive to changing emotion as the surfaces of fair lakes in the wind. There is a passage in Enoch Arden where Annie, impersonated by Lillian Gish, another pupil of Griffith, is waiting in suspense for the return of her husband. She changes from lips of waiting, with a touch of appre-

hension, to a delighted laugh of welcome, her
head making a half-turn toward the door.
The audience is so moved by the beauty of the
slow change they do not know whether her face
is the size of the screen or the size of a postage-
stamp. As a matter of fact it fills the whole
end of the theatre.

Thus much as to faces that are not hieroglyphics. Yet fixed facial hieroglyphics have
many legitimate uses. For instance in The
Avenging Conscience, as the play works toward
the climax and the guilty man is breaking down,
the eye of the detective is thrown on the screen
with all else hid in shadow, a watching, relentless eye. And this suggests a special talis-
man of the old Egyptians, a sign called the
Eyes of Horus, meaning the all-beholding sun.

Here is the picture of an inundated garden:
ﻼﻼ Latin equivalent, the letter S. In our
photoplays the garden is an ever-present resource, and at an instant's necessity suggests
the glory of nature, or sweet privacy, and
kindred things. The Egyptian lotus garden had
to be inundated to be a success. Ours needs
but the hired man with the hose, who sometimes supplies broad comedy. But we turn over
the cardboard, for the deeper meaning of this

hieroglyphic. Our gardens can, as of old, run
the solemn range from those of Babylon to those
of the Resurrection.

If there is one sceptic left as to the hieroglyphic significance of the photoplay, let him
now be discomfited by page fifty-nine, Standard
Dictionary. The last letter in this list is a
lasso: ⟩. The equivalent of the lasso in
the Roman alphabet is the letter T. The
crude and facetious would be apt to suggest
that the equivalent of the lasso in the photoplay is the word trouble, possibly for the hero,
but probably for the villain. We turn to the
other side of the symbol. The noose may stand
for solemn judgment and the hangman, it may
also symbolize the snare of the fowler, temptation. Then there is the spider web, close kin,
representing the cruelty of evolution, in The
Avenging Conscience.

This list is based on the rows of hieroglyphics
most readily at hand. Any volume on Egypt,
such as one of those by Maspero, has a multitude
of suggestions for the man inclined to the idea.

If this system of pasteboard scenarios is
taken literally, I would like to suggest as a
beginning rule that in a play based on twenty
hieroglyphics, nineteen should be the black

realistic signs with obvious meanings, and only
one of them white and inexplicably strange.   It
has been proclaimed further back in this treatise
that there is only one witch in every wood.
And to illustrate further, there is but one
scarlet letter in Hawthorne's story of that name,
but one wine-cup in all of Omar, one Bluebird
in Maeterlinck's play.

I do not insist that the prospective author-
producer adopt the hieroglyphic method as a
routine, if he but consents in his meditative
hours to the point of view that it implies.

The more fastidious photoplay audience
that uses the hieroglyphic hypothesis in an-
alyzing the film before it, will acquire a new
tolerance and understanding of the avalanche
of photoplay conceptions, and find a promise
of beauty in what have been properly classed
as mediocre and stereotyped productions.

The nineteenth chapter has a discourse on
the Book of the Dead. As a connecting link
with that chapter the reader will note that one
of the marked things about the Egyptian wall-
paintings, pictures on the mummy-case wrappings, papyrus inscriptions, and architectural
conceptions, is that they are but enlarged
hieroglyphics, while the hieroglyphics are but

reduced fac-similes of these. So when a few characters are once understood, the highly colored Egyptian wall-paintings of the same things are understood. The hieroglyphic of Osiris is enlarged when they desire to represent him in state. The hieroglyphic of the soul as a human-headed hawk may be in a line of writing no taller than the capitals of this book. Immediately above may be a big painting of the soul, the same hawk placed with the proper care with reference to its composition on the wall, a pure decoration.

The transition from reduction to enlargement and back again is as rapid in Egypt as in the photoplay. It follows, among other things, that in Egypt, as in China and Japan, literary style and mere penmanship and brushwork are to be conceived as inseparable. No doubt the Egyptian scholar was the man who could not only compose a poem, but write it down with a brush. Talent for poetry, deftness in inscribing, and skill in mural painting were probably gifts of the same person. The photoplay goes back to this primitive union in styles.

The stages from hieroglyphics through Phœnician and Greek letters to ours, are of no particular interest here. But the fact that hiero-

glyphics can evolve is important. Let us hope
that our new picture-alphabets can take on
richness and significance, as time goes on, without losing their literal values. They may
develop into something more all-pervading,
yet more highly wrought, than any written
speech. Languages when they evolve produce
stylists, and we will some day distinguish the
different photoplay masters as we now delight
in the separate tang of O. Henry and Mark
Twain and Howells. When these are ancient
times, we will have scholars and critics learned
in the flavors of early moving picture traditions with their histories of movements and
schools, their grammars, and anthologies.

Now some words as to the Anglo-Saxon language and its relation to pictures. In England
and America our plastic arts are but beginning.
Yesterday we were preëminently a word-civilization. England built her mediæval cathedrals,
but they left no legacy among craftsmen. Art
had to lean on imported favorites like Van
Dyck till the days of Sir Joshua Reynolds and the
founding of the Royal Society. Consider that
the friends of Reynolds were of the circle of
Doctor Johnson. Literary tradition had grown
old. Then England had her beginning of land-

scape gardening. Later she saw the rise of Constable, Ruskin, and Turner, and their iridescent successors. Still to-day in England the average leading citizen matches word against word, — using them as algebraic formulas, — rather than picture against picture, when he arranges his thoughts under the eaves of his mind. To step into the Art world is to step out of the beaten path of British dreams. Shakespeare is still king, not Rossetti, nor yet Christopher Wren. Moreover, it was the book-reading colonial who led our rebellion against the very royalty that founded the Academy. The public-speaking American wrote the Declaration of Independence. It was not the work of the painting or cathedral-building Englishman. We were led by Patrick Henry, the orator, Benjamin Franklin, the printer.

The more characteristic America became, the less she had to do with the plastic arts. The emigrant-train carried many a Bible and Dictionary packed in beside the guns and axes. It carried the Elizabethan writers, Æsop's Fables, Blackstone's Commentaries, the revised statutes of Indiana, Bunyan's Pilgrim's Progress, Parson Weems' Life of Washington. But, obviously, there was no place for the Elgin marbles. Giotto's tower could not be loaded in with the dried apples and the seedcorn.

Yesterday morning, though our arts were growing every day, we were still more of a word-civilization than the English. Our architectural, painting, and sculptural history is concerned with men now living, or their immediate predecessors. And even such work as we have is pretty largely a cult by the wealthy. This is the more a cause for misgiving because, in a democracy, the arts, like the political parties, are not founded till they have touched the county chairman, the ward leader, the individual voter. The museums in a democracy should go as far as the public libraries. Every town has its library. There are not twenty Art museums in the land.

Here then comes the romance of the photoplay. A tribe that has thought in words since the days that it worshipped Thor and told legends of the cunning of the tongue of Loki, suddenly begins to think in pictures. The leaders of the people, and of culture, scarcely know the photoplay exists. But in the remote villages the players mentioned in this work are as well known and as fairly understood in their general psychology as any candidates

for president bearing political messages. There
is many a babe in the proletariat not over
four years old who has received more pictures into its eye than it has had words enter
its ear. The young couple go with their first-
born and it sits gaping on its mother's knee.
Often the images are violent and unseemly, a
chaos of rawness and squirm, but scattered
through the experience is a delineation of the
world. Pekin and China, Harvard and Mas-
sachusetts, Portland and Oregon, Benares and
India, become imaginary playgrounds. By
the time the hopeful has reached its geography lesson in the public school it has trav-
elled indeed. Almost any word that means a
picture in the text of the geography or history
or third reader is apt to be translated unconsciously into moving picture terms. In the
next decade, simply from the development of
the average eye, cities akin to the beginnings of
Florence will be born among us as surely as
Chaucer came, upon the first ripening of the
English tongue, after Cædmon and Beowulf.
Sculptors, painters, architects, and park
gardeners who now have their followers by
the hundreds will have admirers by the hundred thousand. The voters will respond to

the aspirations of these artists as the back-
woodsmen followed Poor Richard's Almanac,
or the trappers in their coon-skin caps were
fired to patriotism by Patrick Henry.

This ends the second section of the book.
Were it not for the passage on The Battle
Hymn of the Republic, the chapters thus far
might be entitled : " an open letter to Griffith
and the producers and actors he has trained."
Contrary to my prudent inclinations, he is
the star of the piece, except on one page where
he is the villain. This stardom came about
slowly. In making the final revision, looking
up the producers of the important reels, especially those from the beginning of the photoplay business, numbers of times the photoplays
have turned out to be the work of this former
leading man of Nance O'Neil.

No one can pretend to a full knowledge of the
films. They come faster than rain in April.
It would take a man every day of the year,
working day and night, to see all that come to
Springfield. But in the photoplay world, as I
understand it, D. W. Griffith is the king-figure.

So far, in this work I have endeavored to keep
to the established dogmas of Art. I hope that

the main lines of the argument will appeal to
the people who have classified and related the
beautiful works of man that have preceded the
moving pictures. Let the reader make his own
essay on the subject for the local papers and send
the clipping to me. The next photoplay book
that may appear from this hand may be con-
strued to meet his point of view. It will try to
agree or disagree in clear language. Many a
controversy must come before a method of criticism is fully established.

* * * * * *

At this point I climb from the oracular platform and go down through my own chosen
underbrush for haphazard adventure. I re-
nounce the platform. Whatever it may be
that I find, pawpaw or may-apple or spray
of willow, if you do not want it, throw it
over the edge of the hill, without ado, to the
birds or squirrels or kine, and do not include
it in your controversial discourse. It is not a
part of the dogmatic system of photoplay criticism.

CHAPTER XIV

THE ORCHESTRA, CONVERSATION, AND THE CENSORSHIP

WHENEVER the photoplay is mixed in the same programme with vaudeville, the moving picture part of the show suffers. The film is rushed through, it is battered, it flickers more than commonly, it is a little out of focus. The house is not built for it. The owner of the place cannot manage an art gallery with a circus on his hands. It takes more brains than one man possesses to pick good vaudeville talent and bring good films to the town at the same time. The best motion picture theatres are built for photoplays alone. But they make one mistake.

Almost every motion picture theatre has its orchestra, pianist, or mechanical piano. The perfect photoplay gathering-place would have no sound but the hum of the conversing audience. If this is too ruthless a theory, let the music be played at the intervals between programmes,

while the advertisements are being flung upon
the screen, the lights are on, and the people
coming in.

If there is something more to be done on the
part of the producer to make the film a telling
one, let it be a deeper study of the pictorial
arrangement, with the tones more carefully
balanced, the sculpture vitalized. This is
certainly better than to have a raw thing bul-
lied through with a music-programme, furnished
to bridge the weak places in the construction.
A picture should not be released till it is completely thought out. A producer with this
goal before him will not have the time or brains
to spare to write music that is as closely and
delicately related to the action as the action is
to the background. And unless the tunes are
at one with the scheme they are an intrusion.
Perhaps the moving picture maker has a twin
brother almost as able in music, who possesses
the faculty of subordinating his creations to
the work of his more brilliant coadjutor. How
are they going to make a practical national
distribution of the accompaniment? In the
metropolitan theatres Cabiria carried its own
musicians and programme with a rich if feverish
result. In The Birth of a Nation, music was

used that approached imitative sound devices.
Also the orchestra produced a substitute for
old-fashioned stage suspense by long drawn-
out syncopations. The finer photoplay values
were thrown askew. Perhaps these two per-
formances could be successfully vindicated in
musical policy. But such a defence proves
nothing in regard to the typical film. Imagine
either of these put on in Rochester, Illinois,
population one hundred souls. The reels run
through as well as on Broadway or Michigan
Avenue, but the local orchestra cannot play the
music furnished in annotated sheets as skilfully as the local operator can turn the reel (or
watch the motor turn it!).

The big social fact about the moving picture
is that it is scattered like the newspaper. Any
normal accompaniment thereof must likewise be
adapted to being distributed everywhere. The
present writer has seen, here in his home place,
population sixty thousand, all the films discussed
in this book but Cabiria and The Birth of a
Nation. It is a photoplay paradise, the spoken
theatre is practically banished. Unfortunately
the local moving picture managers think it
necessary to have orchestras. The musicians
they can secure make tunes that are most

squalid and horrible. With fathomless imbecility, hoochey koochey strains are on the air while heroes are dying. The Miserere is in our ears when the lovers are reconciled. Ragtime is imposed upon us while the old mother prays for her lost boy. Sometimes the musician with this variety of sympathy abandons himself to thrilling improvisation.

My thoughts on this subject began to take form several years ago, when the film this book has much praised, The Battle Hymn of the Republic, came to town. The proprietor of one theatre put in front of his shop a twenty-foot sign "The Battle Hymn of the Republic, by Harriet Beecher Stowe, brought back by special request." He had probably read Julia Ward Howe's name on the film forty times before the sign went up. His assistant, I presume his daughter, played "In the Shade of the Old Apple Tree" hour after hour, while the great film was rolling by. Many old soldiers were coming to see it. I asked the assistant why she did not play and sing the Battle Hymn. She said they "just couldn't find it." Are the distributors willing to send out a musician with each film?

Many of the Springfield producers are quite

able and enterprising, but to ask for music with photoplays is like asking the man at the news stand to write an editorial while he sells you the paper. The picture with a great orchestra in a far-off metropolitan Opera House, may be classed by fanatic partisanship with Grand Opera. But few can get at it. It has nothing to do with Democracy.

Of course people with a mechanical imagination, and no other kind, begin to suggest the talking moving picture at this point, or the phonograph or the mechanical piano. Let us discuss the talking moving picture only. That disposes of the others.

If the talking moving picture becomes a reliable mirror of the human voice and frame, it will be the basis of such a separate art that none of the photoplay precedents will apply. It will be the *phonoplay*, not the photoplay. It will be unpleasant for a long time. This book is a struggle against the non-humanness of the undisciplined photograph. Any film is correct, realistic, forceful, many times before it is charming. The actual physical storage-battery of the actor is many hundred miles away. As a substitute, the human quality must come in the marks of the presence of the producer. The entire painting must have his brush-work. If we compare it to a love-letter it must be in his handwriting rather than worked on a typewriter. If he puts his autograph into the film, it is after a fierce struggle with the uncanny scientific quality of the camera's work. His genius and that of the whole company of actors is exhausted in the task.

The raw phonograph is likewise unmagnetic. Would you set upon the shoulders of the troupe of actors the additional responsibility of putting an adequate substitute for human magnetism in the phonographic disk? The voice that does not actually bleed, that contains no heart-beats, fails to meet the emergency. Few people have wept over a phonographic selection from Tristan and Isolde. They are moved at the actual performance. Why? Look at the opera singer after the last act. His eyes are burning. His face is flushed. His pulse is high. Reaching his hotel room, he is far more weary than if he had sung the opera alone there. He has given out of his brain-fire and blood-beat the same magnetism that leads men in battle. To speak of it in the crassest terms, this resource brings him a hundred times more salary than another man with just as good a voice can command. The output that leaves him drained at the end of the show cannot be stored in the phonograph machine. That device is as good in the morning as at noon. It ticks like a clock.

To perfect the talking moving picture, human magnetism must be put into the mirror-screen and into the clock. Not only is this imperative, but clock and mirror must be harmonized, one gently subordinated to the other. Both cannot rule. In the present talking moving picture the more highly developed photoplay is dragged by the hair in a dead faint, in the wake of the screaming savage phonograph. No talking machine on the market reproduces conversation clearly unless it be elaborately articulated in unnatural tones with a stiff interval between each question and answer. Real dialogue goes to ruin.

The talking moving picture came to our town. We were given for one show a line of minstrels facing the audience, with the interlocutor repeating his immemorial question, and the end-man giving the immemorial answer. Then came a scene in a blacksmith shop where certain well-differentiated rackets were carried over the footlights. No one heard the blacksmith, unless he stopped to shout straight at us.

The *phonoplay* can quite possibly reach some divine goal, but it will be after the speaking powers of the phonograph excel the photographing powers of the reel, and then the pictures will be brought in as comment and ornament to the speech. The pictures will be held back by the phonograph as long as it is more limited in its range. The pictures are at present freer and more versatile without it. If the *phonoplay* is ever established, since it will double the machinery, it must needs double its prices. It will be the illustrated phonograph, in a more expensive theatre.

The orchestra is in part a blundering effort by the local manager to supply the human-magnetic element which he feels lacking in the pictures on which the producer has not left his autograph. But there is a much more economic and magnetic accompaniment, the before-mentioned buzzing commentary of the audience. There will be some people who disturb the neighbors in front, but the average crowd has developed its manners in this particular, and when the orchestra is silent, murmurs like a pleasant brook.

Local manager, why not an advertising campaign in your town that says: "Beginning Monday and henceforth, ours shall be known as the Conversational Theatre"? At the door let each person be handed the following card:—

"You are encouraged to discuss the picture with the friend who accompanies you to this place. Conversation, of course, must be sufficiently subdued not to disturb the stranger who did not come with you to the theatre. If you are so disposed, consider your answers to these questions: What play or part of a play given in this theatre did you like most to-day? What the least? What is the best picture you have ever seen anywhere? What pictures, seen here this month, shall we bring back?" Here give a list of the recent productions, with squares to mark by the Australian ballot system: approved or disapproved. The cards with their answers could be slipped into the ballot-box at the door as the crowd goes out.

It may be these questions are for the exceptional audiences in residence districts. Perhaps with most crowds the last interrogation is the only one worth while. But by gathering habitually the answers to that alone the place would get the drift of its public, realize its genius, and become an art-gallery, the people bestowing the blue ribbons. The photoplay theatres have coupon contests and balloting already : the most popular young lady, money prizes to the best vote-getter in the audience, etc. Why not ballot on the matter in hand?

If the cards are sent out by the big producers, a referendum could be secured that would be invaluable in arguing down to rigid censorship, and enable them to make their own private censorship more intelligent. Various styles of experimental cards could be tried till the vital one is found.

There is growing up in this country a clan of half-formed moving picture critics. The present stage of their work is indicated by the eloquent notice describing Your Girl and Mine, in the chapter on " Progress and Endowment." The metropolitan papers give their photoplay reporters as much space as the theatrical critics. Here in my home town the twelve moving picture places take one half a page of chaotic notices daily. The country is being badly led by professional photoplay newswriters who do not know where they are going, but are on the way.

But they aptly describe the habitual attendants as moving picture fans. The fan at the photoplay, as at the base-ball grounds, is neither a low-brow nor a high-brow. He is an enthusiast who is as stirred by the charge of the photographic cavalry as by the home runs that he watches from the bleachers. In both places he has the privilege of comment while the game goes on. In the photoplay theatre it is not so vociferous, but as keenly felt. Each person roots by himself. He has his own judgment, and roasts the umpire: who is the keeper of the local theatre: or the producer, as the case may be. If these opinions of the fan can be collected and classified, an informal censorship is at once established. The photoplay reporters can then take the enthusiasts in hand and lead them to a realization of the finer points in awarding praise and blame. Even the sporting pages have their expert opinions with due influence on the betting odds. Out of the work of the photoplay reporters let a superstructure of art criticism be reared in periodicals like The Century, Harper's, Scribner's, The Atlantic, The Craftsman, and the architectural magazines. These are our natural custodians of art. They should reproduce the most exquisite tableaus, and be as fastidious in their selection of them as they are in the current examples of the other arts. Let them spread the news when photoplays keyed to the Rembrandt mood arrive. The reporters for the newspapers should get their ideas and refreshment in such places as the Ryerson Art Library of the Chicago Art Institute. They should begin with such books as Richard Muther's History of Modern Painting, John C. Van Dyke's Art for Art's Sake, Marquand and Frothingham's History of Sculpture, A. D. F. Hamlin's History of Architecture. They should take the business of guidance in this new world as a sacred trust, knowing they have the power to influence an enormous democracy.

The moving picture journals and the literati are in straits over the censorship question. The literati side with the managers, on the principles of free speech and a free press. But few of the æsthetically super-wise are persistent fans. They rave for freedom, but are not, as a general thing, living back in the home town. They do not face the exigency of having their summer and winter amusement spoiled day after day.

Extremists among the pious are railing against the moving pictures as once they railed against novels. They have no notion

that this institution is penetrating to the last
backwoods of our civilization, where its presence is as hard to prevent as the rain. But
some of us are destined to a reaction, almost
as strong as the obsession. The religionists
will think they lead it. They will be self-
deceived. Moving picture nausea is already
taking hold of numberless people, even when
they are in the purely pagan mood. Forced
by their limited purses, their inability to buy
a Ford car, and the like, they go in their loneli-
ness to film after film till the whole world seems
to turn on a reel. When they are again at home,
they see in the dark an imaginary screen with
tremendous pictures, whirling by at a horribly
accelerated pace, a photoplay delirium tremens.
Faster and faster the reel turns in the back of
their heads. When the moving picture sea-sickness is upon one, nothing satisfies but the quietest
out of doors, the companionship of the gentlest
of real people. The non-movie-life has charms
such as one never before conceived. The worn
citizen feels that the cranks and legislators can
do what they please to the producers. He is
through with them.

The moving picture business men do not
realize that they have to face these nervous

conditions in their erstwhile friends. They
flatter themselves they are being pursued by
some reincarnations of Anthony Comstock.
There are several reasons why photoplay corporations are callous, along with the sufficient
one that they are corporations.

First, they are engaged in a financial orgy.
Fortunes are being found by actors and managers faster than they were dug up in 1849 and
1850 in California. Forty-niner lawlessness of
soul prevails. They talk each other into a
lordly state of mind. All is dash and experiment. Look at the advertisements in the
leading moving picture magazines. They are
like the praise of oil stock or Peruna. They
bawl about films founded upon little classics.
They howl about plots that are ostensibly from
the soberest of novels, whose authors they blas-
phemously invoke. They boo and blow about
twisted, callous scenarios that are bad imita-
tions of the world's most beloved lyrics.

The producers do not realize the mass effect
of the output of the business. It appears to
many as a sea of unharnessed photography:
sloppy conceptions set forth with sharp edges
and irrelevant realism. The jumping, twitching, cold-blooded devices, day after day, create

the aforesaid sea-sickness, that has nothing to do with the questionable subject. When on top of this we come to the picture that is actually insulting, we are up in arms indeed. It is supplied by a corporation magnate removed from his audience in location, fortune, interest, and mood: an absentee landlord. I was trying to convert a talented and noble friend to the films. The first time we went there was a prize-fight between a black and a white man, not advertised, used for a filler. I said it was queer, and would not happen again. The next time my noble friend was persuaded to go, there was a cock-fight, incidental to a Cuban romance. The third visit we beheld a lady who was dying for five minutes, rolling her eyes about in a way that was fearful to see. The convert was not made.

It is too easy to produce an unprovoked murder, an inexplicable arson, neither led up to nor followed by the ordinary human history of such acts, and therefore as arbitrary as the deeds of idiots or the insane. A villainous hate, an alleged love, a violent death, are flashed at us, without being in any sort of tableau logic. The public is ceaselessly played upon by tactless devices. Therefore it howls, just as children in the nursery do when the awkward governess tries the very thing the diplomatic governess, in reasonable time, may bring about.

The producer has the man in the audience who cares for the art peculiarly at his mercy. Compare him with the person who wants to read a magazine for an evening. He can look over all the periodicals in the local book-store in fifteen minutes. He can select the one he wants, take this bit of printed matter home, go through the contents, find the three articles he prefers, get an evening of reading out of them, and be happy. Every day as many photoplays come to our town as magazines come to the book-store in a week or a month. There are good ones and bad ones buried in the list. There is no way to sample the films. One has to wait through the first third of a reel before he has an idea of the merits of a production, his ten cents is spent, and much of his time is gone. It would take five hours at least to find the best film in our town for one day. Meanwhile, nibbling and sampling, the seeker would run such a gantlet of plot and dash and chase that his eyes and patience would be exhausted. Recently there returned to the city for a day one of Griffith's best Biographs, The Last Drop of Water. It was good to see again. In order to watch this one reel twice I had to wait through five others of unutterable miscellany.

Since the producers and theatre-managers have us at their mercy, they are under every obligation to consider our delicate susceptibilities — granting the proposition that in an ideal world we will have no legal censorship. As to what to do in this actual nation, let the reader follow what John Collier has recently written in The Survey. Collier was the leading force in founding the National Board of Censorship. As a member of that volunteer extra-legal board which is independent and high minded, yet accepted by the leading picture companies, he is able to discuss legislation in a manner which the present writer cannot hope to match. Read John Collier. But I wish to suggest that the ideal censorship is that to which the daily press is subject, the elastic hand of public opinion, if the photoplay can be brought as near to newspaper conditions in this matter as it is in some others.

How does public opinion grip the journalist? The editor has a constant report from his constituency. A popular scoop sells an extra

at once.   An attack on the wrong idol cancels
fifty subscriptions.   People come to the office
to do it, and say why.   If there is a piece of
real news on the second page, and fifty letters
come in about it that night, next month
when that character of news reappears it gets
the front page.   Some human peculiarities are
not mentioned, some phrases not used.   The
total attribute of the blue-pencil man is diplomacy.   But while the motion pictures come out
every day, they get their discipline months afterwards in the legislation that insists on everything
but tact.   A tentative substitute for the letters
that come to the editor, the personal call and
cancelled subscription, and the rest, is the
system of balloting on the picture, especially
the answer to the question, "What picture seen
here this month, or this week, shall we bring
back?"   Experience will teach how to put
the queries.   By the same system the public
might dictate its own cut-outs.   Let us have
a democracy and a photoplay business working in daily rhythm.

CHAPTER XV

THE SUBSTITUTE FOR THE SALOON

THIS is a special commentary on chapter five, The Picture of Crowd Splendor. It refers as well to every other type of moving picture that gets into the slum. But the masses have an extraordinary affinity for the Crowd Photoplay. As has been said before, the mob comes nightly to behold its natural face in the glass. Politicians on the platform have swayed the mass below them. But now, to speak in an Irish way, the crowd takes the platform, and looking down, sees itself swaying. The slums are an astonishing assembly of cave-men crawling out of their shelters to exhibit for the first time in history a common interest on a tremendous scale in an art form. Below the cliff caves were bar rooms in endless lines. There are almost as many bar rooms to-day, yet this new thing breaks the lines as nothing else ever did. Often when a moving picture house is set up, the saloon on the right hand or the left declares bankruptcy.

Why do men prefer the photoplay to the drinking place? For no pious reason, surely. Now they have fire pouring into their eyes instead of into their bellies. Blood is drawn from the guts to the brain. Though the picture be the veriest mess, the light and movement cause the beholder to do a little reptilian thinking. After a day's work a street-sweeper enters the place, heavy as King Log. A ditch-digger goes in, sick and surly. It is the state of the body when many men drink themselves into insensibility. But here the light is as strong in the eye as whiskey in the throat. Along with the flare, shadow, and mystery, they face the existence of people, places, costumes, utterly novel. Immigrants are prodded by these swords of darkness and light to guess at the meaning of the catch-phrases and headlines that punctuate the play. They strain to hear their neighbors whisper or spell them out.

The photoplays have done something to reunite the lower-class families. No longer is the fire-escape the only summer resort for big and little folks. Here is more fancy and whim than ever before blessed a hot night. Here, under the wind of an electric fan, they witness everything, from a burial in Westminster to the

birthday parade of the ruler of the land of
Swat.

The usual saloon equipment to delight the
eye is one so-called "leg" picture of a woman,
a photograph of a prize-fighter, and some
colored portraits of goats to advertise various
brands of beer. Many times, no doubt, these
boys and young men have found visions of a
sordid kind while gazing on the actress, the
fighter, or the goats. But what poor material
they had in the wardrobes of memory for the
trimmings and habiliments of vision, to make
this lady into Freya, this prize-fighter into
Thor, these goats into the harnessed steeds
that drew his chariot! Man's dreams are re-
arranged and glorified memories. How could
these people reconstruct the torn carpets and
tin cans and waste-paper of their lives into mythology? How could memories of Ladies' Entrance squalor be made into Castles in Granada
or Carcassonne? The things they drank to see,
and saw but grotesquely, and paid for terribly,
now roll before them with no after pain or punishment. The mumbled conversation, the socia-
bility for which they leaned over the tables, they
have here in the same manner with far more
to talk about. They come, they go home, men

and women together, as casually and impulsively
as the men alone ever entered a drinking-place,
but discoursing now of far-off mountains and
star-crossed lovers.   As Padraic Colum says in
his poem on the herdsman : —

> "With thoughts on white ships
> And the King of Spain's Daughter."

This is why the saloon on the right hand and
on the left in the slum is apt to move out when
the photoplay moves in.

But let us go to the other end of the temperance argument.   I beg to be allowed to relate a
personal matter.   For some time I was a field-
worker for the Anti-Saloon League of Illinois,
being sent every Sunday to a new region to
make the yearly visit on behalf of the league.
Such a visitor is apt to speak to one church in a
village, and two in the country, on each excur-
sion, being met at the station by some leading
farmer-citizen of the section, and driven to these
points by him.   The talk with this man was
worth it all to me.

The agricultural territory of the United States
is naturally dry.   This is because the cross-roads
church is the only communal institution, and
the voice of the cross-roads pastor is for teeto-

talism.   The routine of the farm-hand, while by
no means ideal in other respects, keeps him from
craving drink as intensely as other toilers do.
A day's work in the open air fills his veins at
nightfall with an opiate of weariness instead of a
high-strung nervousness.   The strong men of
the community are church elders, not through
fanaticism, but by right of leadership.   Through
their office they are committed to prohibition.
So opposition to the temperance movement is
scattering.   The Anti-Saloon League has organ-
ized these leaders into a nation-wide machine.
It sees that they get their weekly paper, instruct-
ing them in the tactics whereby local fights have
been won.   A subscription financing the State
League is taken once a year.   It counts on the
regular list of church benevolences.   The state
officers come in to help on the critical local
fights.   Any country politician fears their
non-partisan denunciation as he does political
death.   The local machines thus backed are
incurable mugwumps, hold the balance of
power, work in both parties, and have voted
dry the agricultural territory of the United
States everywhere, by the township, county,
or state unit.

The only institutions that touch the same

territory in a similar way are the Chautauquas in the prosperous agricultural centres. These, too, by the same sign are emphatically anti-saloon in their propaganda, serving to intellectualize and secularize the dry sentiment without taking it out of the agricultural caste.

There is a definite line between our farm-civilization and the rest. When a county goes dry, it is generally in spite of the county-seat. Such temperance people as are in the court-house town represent the church-vote, which is even then in goodly proportion a retired-farmer vote. The larger the county-seat, the larger the non-church-going population and the more stubborn the fight. The majority of miners and factory workers are on the wet side everywhere. The irritation caused by the gases in the mines, by the dirty work in the blackness, by the squalor in which the company houses are built, turns men to drink for reaction and lamplight and comradeship. The similar fevers and exasperations of factory life lead the workers to unstring their tense nerves with liquor. The habit of snuggling up close in factories, conversing often, bench by bench, machine by machine, inclines them to get together for their pleasures at the bar.

In industrial America there is an anti-saloon minority in moral sympathy with the temperance wave brought in by the farmers. But they are outstanding groups. Their leadership seldom dries up a factory town or a mining region, with all the help the Anti-Saloon League can give.

In the big cities the temperance movement is scarcely understood. The choice residential districts are voted dry for real estate reasons. The men who do this, drink freely at their own clubs or parties. The temperance question would be fruitlessly argued to the end of time were it not for the massive agricultural vote rolling and roaring round each metropolis, reawakening the town churches whose vote is a pitiful minority but whose spokesmen are occasionally strident.

There is a prophecy abroad that prohibition will be the issue of a national election. If the question is squarely put, there are enough farmers and church-people to drive the saloon out of legal existence. The women's vote, a little more puritanical than the men's vote, will make the result sure. As one anxious for this victory, I have often speculated on the situation when all America is nominally dry, at the behest of the American farmer, the American preacher, and the American woman. When the use of alcohol is treason, what will become of those all but unbroken lines of slum saloons? No lesser force than regular troops could dislodge them, with yesterday's intrenchment.

The entrance of the motion picture house into the arena is indeed striking, the first enemy of King Alcohol with real power where that king has deepest hold. If every one of those saloon doors is nailed up by the Chautauqua orators, the photoplay archway will remain open. The people will have a shelter where they can readjust themselves, that offers a substitute for many of the lines of pleasure in the groggery. And a whole evening costs but a dime apiece. Several rounds of drinks are expensive, but the people can sit through as many repetitions of this programme as they desire, for one entrance fee. The dominant genius of the moving picture place is not a gentleman with a red nose and an eye like a dead fish, but some producer who, with all his faults, has given every person in the audience a seven-leagued angel-and-demon telescope.

Since I have announced myself a farmer and

a puritan, let me here list the saloon evils not
yet recorded in this chapter. They are separate
from the catalogue of the individualistic woes of
the drunkard that are given in the Scripture.
The shame of the American drinking place
is the bar-tender who dominates its thinking.
His cynical and hardened soul wipes out a
portion of the influence of the public school,
the library, the self-respecting newspaper. A
stream rises no higher than its source, and
through his dead-fish eye and dead-fish brain
the group of tired men look upon all the statesmen and wise ones of the land. Though he
says worse than nothing, his furry tongue, by
endless reiteration, is the American slum oracle.
At the present the bar-tender handles the
neighborhood group, the ultimate unit in city
politics.

So, good citizen, welcome the coming of the
moving picture man as a local social force.
Whatever his private character, the mere
formula of his activities makes him a better
type. He may not at first sway his group
in a directly political way, but he will make
himself the centre of more social ideals than
the bar-tender ever entertained. And he is
beginning to have as intimate a relation to

his public as the bar-tender. In many cases he stands under his arch in the sheltered lobby and is on conversing terms with his habitual customers, the length of the afternoon and evening.

Voting the saloon out of the slums by voting America dry, does not, as of old, promise to be a successful operation that kills the patient. In the past some of the photoplay magazines have contained denunciations of the temperance people for refusing to say anything in behalf of the greatest practical enemy of the saloon. But it is not too late for the dry forces to repent. The Anti-Saloon League officers and the photoplay men should ask each other to dinner. More moving picture theatres in doubtful territory will help make dry voters. And wet territory voted dry will bring about a greatly accelerated patronage of the photoplay houses. There is every strategic reason why these two forces should patch up a truce.

Meanwhile, the cave-man, reader of picture-writing, is given a chance to admit light into his mind, whatever he puts to his lips. Let us look for the day, be it a puritan triumph or not, when the sons and the daughters of the slums shall prophesy, the young men shall see visions, the old men dream dreams.

CHAPTER XVI

CALIFORNIA AND AMERICA

THE moving picture captains of industry, like the California gold finders of 1849, making colossal fortunes in two or three years, have the same glorious irresponsibility and occasional need of the sheriff. They are Californians more literally than this. Around Los Angeles the greatest and most characteristic moving picture colonies are being built. Each photoplay magazine has its California letter, telling of the putting-up of new studios, and the transfer of actors, with much slap-you-on-the-back personal gossip. This is the outgrowth of the fact that every type of the photoplay but the intimate is founded on some phase of the out-of-doors. Being thus dependent, the plant can best be set up where there is no winter. Besides this, the Los Angeles region has the sea, the mountains, the desert, and many kinds of grove and field. Landscape and architecture are sub-tropical. But for a description of

California, ask any traveller or study the background of almost any photoplay.

If the photoplay is the consistent utterance of its scenes, if the actors are incarnations of the land they walk upon, as they should be, California indeed stands a chance to achieve through the films an utterance of her own. Will this land furthest west be the first to capture the inner spirit of this newest and most curious of the arts? It certainly has the opportunity that comes with the actors, producers, and equipment. Let us hope that every region will develop the silent photographic pageant in a local form as outlined in the chapter on Progress and Endowment. Already the California sort, in the commercial channels, has become the broadly accepted if mediocre national form. People who revere the Pilgrim Fathers of 1620 have often wished those gentlemen had moored their bark in the region of Los Angeles rather than Plymouth Rock, that Boston had been founded there. At last that landing is achieved.

Patriotic art students have discussed with mingled irony and admiration the Boston domination of the only American culture of the nineteenth century, namely, literature.

Indianapolis has had her day since then, Chicago is lifting her head. Nevertheless Boston still controls the text-book in English and dominates our high schools. Ironic feelings in this matter on the part of western men are based somewhat on envy and illegitimate cussedness, but are also grounded in the honest hope of a healthful rivalry. They want new romanticists and artists as indigenous to their soil as was Hawthorne to witch-haunted Salem or Longfellow to the chestnuts of his native heath. Whatever may be said of the patriarchs, from Oliver Wendell Holmes to Amos Bronson Alcott, they were true sons of the New England stone fences and meeting houses. They could not have been born or nurtured anywhere else on the face of the earth.

Some of us view with a peculiar thrill the prospect that Los Angeles may become the Boston of the photoplay. Perhaps it would be better to say the Florence, because California reminds one of colorful Italy more than of any part of the United States. Yet there is a difference.

The present-day man-in-the-street, man-about-town Californian has an obvious magnificence about him that is allied to the eucalyptus tree, the pomegranate. California is a gilded state. It has not the sordidness of gold, as has Wall Street, but it is the embodiment of the natural ore that the ragged prospector finds. The gold of California is the color of the orange, the glitter of dawn in the Yosemite, the hue of the golden gate that opens the sunset way to mystic and terrible Cathay and Hindustan.

The enemy of California says the state is magnificent but thin. He declares it is as though it were painted on a Brobdingnagian piece of gilt paper, and he who dampens his finger and thrusts it through finds an alkali valley on the other side, the lonely prickly pear, and a heap of ashes from a deserted campfire. He says the citizens of this state lack the richness of an æsthetic and religious tradition. He says there is no substitute for time. But even these things make for coincidence. This apparent thinness California has in common with the routine photoplay, which is at times as shallow in its thought as the shadow it throws upon the screen. This newness California has in common with all photoplays. It is thrillingly possible for the state and the art to acquire spiritual tradition and depth together.

Part of the thinness of California is not only
its youth, but the result of the physical fact
that the human race is there spread over so
many acres of land. They try not only to
count their mines and enumerate their palm
trees, but they count the miles of their sea-
coast, and the acres under cultivation and the
height of the peaks, and revel in large statistics
and the bigness generally, and forget how a few
men rattle around in a great deal of scenery.
They shout their statistics across the Rockies
and the deserts to New York. The Mississippi
Valley is non-existent to the Californian. His
fellow-feeling is for the opposite coast-line.
Through the geographical accident of separa-
tion by mountain and desert from the rest of
the country, he becomes a mere shouter, hurrah-
ing so assiduously that all variety in the voice
is lost. Then he tries gestures, and becomes
flamboyant, rococo.

These are the defects of the motion picture
qualities also. Its panoramic tendency runs
wild. As an institution it advertises itself
with the sweeping gesture. It has the same
passion for coast-line. These are not the sins
of New England. When, in the hands of
masters, they become sources of strength, they

will be a different set of virtues from those of
New England.

There is no more natural place for the scattering of confetti than this state, except the
moving picture scene itself. Both have a genius
for gardens and dancing and carnival.

When the Californian relegates the dramatic
to secondary scenes, both in his life and his
photoplay, and turns to the genuinely epic
and lyric, he and this instrument may find their
immortality together as New England found
its soul in the essays of Emerson. Tide upon
tide of Spring comes into California through
all four seasons. Fairy beauty overwhelms
the lumbering grand-stand players. The tiniest
garden is a jewelled pathway of wonder. But
the Californian cannot shout "orange blossoms,
orange blossoms; heliotrope, heliotrope!" He
cannot boom forth "roseleaves, roseleaves" so
that he does their beauties justice. Here is
where the photoplay can begin to give him a
more delicate utterance. And he can go on
into stranger things and evolve all the Splendor
Films into higher types, for the very name of
California is splendor. The California photoplaywright can base his Crowd Picture upon
the city-worshipping mobs of San Francisco.

He can derive his Patriotic and Religious Splendors from something older and more magnificent than the aisles of the Romanesque, namely: the groves of the giant redwoods.

The campaign for a beautiful nation could very well emanate from the west coast, where with the slightest care grow up models for all the world of plant arrangement and tree-luxury. Our mechanical East is reproved, our tension is relaxed, our ugliness is challenged every time we look upon those garden paths and forests.

It is possible for Los Angeles to lay hold of the motion picture as our national text-book in Art as Boston appropriated to herself the guardianship of the national text-books of Literature. If California has a shining soul, and not merely a golden body, let her forget her seventeen-year-old melodramatics, and turn to her poets who understand the heart underneath the glory. Edwin Markham, the dean of American singers, Clark Ashton Smith, the young star treader, George Sterling, that son of Ancient Merlin, have in their songs the seeds of better scenarios than California has sent us. There are two poems by George Sterling that I have had in mind for many a day as conceptions that should inspire mystic films akin to them. These poems are The Night Sentries and Tidal King of Nations.

But California can tell us stories that are grim children of the tales of the wild Ambrose Bierce. Then there is the lovely unforgotten Nora May French and the austere Edward Rowland Sill.

Edison is the new Gutenberg. He has invented the new printing. The state that realizes this may lead the soul of America, day after to-morrow.

CHAPTER XVII

PROGRESS AND ENDOWMENT

THE moving picture goes almost as far as journalism into the social fabric in some ways, further in others. Soon, no doubt, many a little town will have its photographic news-press. We have already the weekly world-news films from the big centres.

With local journalism will come devices for advertising home enterprises. Some staple products will be made attractive by having film-actors show their uses. The motion pictures will be in the public schools to stay. Text-books in geography, history, zoölogy, botany, physiology, and other sciences will be illustrated by standardized films. Along with these changes, there will be available at certain centres collections of films equivalent to the Standard Dictionary and the Encyclopædia Britannica.

And sooner or later we will have a straight-out capture of a complete film expression by the serious forces of civilization. The merely impudent motion picture will be relegated to the leisure hours with yellow journalism. Photoplay libraries are inevitable, as active if not as multitudinous as the book-circulating libraries. The oncoming machinery and expense of the motion picture is immense. Where will the money come from? No one knows. What the people want they will get. The race of man cannot afford automobiles, but has them nevertheless. We cannot run away into non-automobile existence or non-steam-engine or non-movie life long at a time. We must conquer this thing. While the more stately scientific and educational aspects just enumerated are slowly on their way, the artists must be up and about their ameliorative work.

Every considerable effort to develop a noble idiom will count in the final result, as the writers of early English made possible the language of the Bible, Shakespeare, and Milton. We are perfecting a medium to be used as long as Chinese ideographs have been. It will no doubt, like the Chinese language, record in the end massive and classical treatises, imperial chronicles, law-codes, traditions, and religious admonitions. All this by the *motion picture* as a recording instrument, not necessarily the *photoplay*, a much more limited thing, a form of art.

What shall be done in especial by this generation of idealists, whose flags rise and go down, whose battle line wavers and breaks a thousand times? What is the high quixotic splendid call? We know of a group of public-spirited people who advocate, in endowed films, "safety first," another that champions total abstinence. Often their work seems lost in the mass of commercial production, but it is a good beginning. Such citizens take an established studio for a specified time and at the end put on the market a production that backs up their particular idea. There are certain terms between the owners of the film and the proprietors of the studio for the division of the income, the profits of the cult being spent on further propaganda. The product need not necessarily be the type outlined in chapter two, The Photoplay of Action. Often some other sort might establish the cause more deeply. But most of the propaganda films are of the action variety, because of the dynamic character of the people who produce them. Fired by fanatic zeal, the auto speeds faster, the rescuing hero runs harder, the stern policeman and sheriff become more jumpy, all that the audience may be converted. Here if anywhere meditation on the actual resources of charm and force in the art is a fitting thing. The crusader should realize that it is not a good Action Play nor even a good argument unless it is indeed the Winged Victory sort. The gods are not always on the side of those who throw fits.

There is here appended a newspaper description of a crusading film, that, despite the implications of the notice, has many passages of charm. It is two-thirds Action Photoplay, one-third Intimate-and-friendly. The notice does not imply that at times the story takes pains to be gentle. This bit of writing is all too typical of film journalism.

"Not only as an argument for suffrage but as a play with a story, a punch, and a mission, 'Your Girl and Mine' is produced under the direction of the National Woman's Suffrage Association at the Capitol to-day.

"Olive Wyndham forsook the legitimate stage for the time to pose as the heroine of the play. Katherine Kaelred, leading lady of 'Joseph and his Brethren,' took the part of a woman lawyer battling for the right. Sydney

Booth, of the 'Yellow Ticket' company posed as the hero of the experiment. John Charles and Katharine Henry played the villain and the honest working girl. About three hundred secondaries were engaged along with the principals.

"It is melodrama of the most thrilling sort, in spite of the fact that there is a moral concealed in the very title of the play. But who is worried by a moral in a play which has an exciting hand-to-hand fight between a man and a woman in one of the earliest acts, when the quick march of events ranges from a wedding to a murder and an automobile abduction scene that breaks all former speed-records. 'The Cause' comes in most symbolically and poetically, a symbolic figure that 'fades out' at critical periods in the plot. Dr. Anna Howard Shaw, the famous suffrage leader, appears personally in the film.

"'Your Girl and Mine' is a big play with a big mission built on a big scale. It is a whole evening's entertainment, and a very interesting evening at that." Here endeth the newspaper notice. Compare it with the Biograph advertisement of Judith in chapter six.

There is nothing in the film that rasps like

this account of it. The clipping serves to give the street-atmosphere through which our Woman's Suffrage Joan of Arcs move to conquest and glory with unstained banners.

The obvious amendments to the production as an instrument of persuasion are two. Firstly there should be five reels instead of six, every scene shortened a bit to bring this result. Secondly, the lieutenant governor of the state, who is the Rudolf Rassendyll of the production, does not enter the story soon enough, and is too James K. Hacketty all at once. We are jerked into admiration of him, rather than ensnared. But after that the gentleman behaves more handsomely than any of the distinguished lieutenant governors in real life the present writer happens to remember. The figure of Aunt Jane, the queenly serious woman of affairs, is one to admire and love. Her effectiveness without excess or strain is in itself an argument for giving woman the vote. The newspaper notice does not state the facts in saying the symbolical figure "fades out" at critical periods in the plot. On the contrary, she appears at critical periods, clothed in white, solemn and royal. She comes into the groups with an adequate allurement, pointing the moral

of each situation while she shines brightest.
The two children for whom the contest is fought
are winsome little girls. By the side of their
mother in the garden or in the nursery they
are a potent argument for the natural rights
of femininity. The film is by no means ultra-
æsthetic. The implications of the clipping are
correct to that degree. But the resources of
beauty within the ready command of the ad-
vising professional producer are used by the
women for all they are worth. It could not
be asked of them that they evolve technical
novelties.

Yet the figures of Aunt Jane and the Goddess
of Suffrage are something new in their fashion.
Aunt Jane is a spiritual sister to that unprec-
edented woman, Jane Addams, who went to
the Hague conference for Peace in the midst of
war, which heroic action the future will not
forget. Aunt Jane does justice to that breed
of women amid the sweetness and flowers and
mere scenario perils of the photoplay story. The
presence of the "Votes for Women" figure is
the beginning of a line of photoplay goddesses
that serious propaganda in the new medium
will make part of the American Spiritual
Hierarchy. In the imaginary film of Our

Lady Springfield, described in the chapter on Architecture-in-Motion, a kindred divinity is presumed to stand by the side of the statue when it first reaches the earth.

High-minded graduates of university courses in sociology and schools of philanthropy, devout readers of The Survey, The Chicago Public, The Masses, The New Republic, La Follette's, are going to advocate increasingly, their varied and sometimes contradictory causes, in films. These will generally be produced by heroic exertions in the studio, and much passing of the subscription paper outside.

Then there are endowments already in existence that will no doubt be diverted to the photoplay channel. In every state house, and in Washington, D.C., increasing quantities of dead printed matter have been turned out year after year. They have served to kindle various furnaces and feed the paper-mills a second time. Many of these routine reports will remain in innocuous desuetude. But one-fourth of them, perhaps, are capable of being embodied in films. If they are scientific demonstrations, they can be made into realistic motion picture records. If they are exhortations, they can be transformed into plays with a moral, brothers of the film Your Girl and Mine. The appropriations for public printing should include such work hereafter.

The scientific museums distribute routine pamphlets that would set the whole world right on certain points if they were but read by said world. Let them be filmed and started. Whatever the congressman is permitted to frank to his constituency, let him send in the motion picture form when it is the expedient and expressive way.

When men work for the high degrees in the universities, they labor on a piece of literary conspiracy called a thesis which no one outside the university hears of again. The gist of this research work that is dead to the democracy, through the university merits of thoroughness, moderation of statement, and final touch of discovery, would have a chance to live and grip the people in a motion picture transcript, if not a photoplay. It would be University Extension. The relentless fire of criticism which the heads of the departments would pour on the production before they allowed it to pass would result in a standardization of the sense of scientific fact over the land. Suppose the film has

the coat of arms of the University of Chicago
along with the name of the young graduate
whose thesis it is. He would have a chance
to reflect credit on the university even as much
as a foot-ball player.

Large undertakings might be under way, like
those described in the chapter on Architecture-
in-Motion. But these would require much
more than the ordinary outlay for thesis
work, less, perhaps, than is taken for Athletics.
Lyman Howe and several other world-explorers
have already set the pace in the more human side of the educative film. The list of
Mr. Howe's offerings from the first would
reveal many a one that would have run the
gantlet of a university department. He
points out a new direction for old energies,
whereby professors may become citizens.

Let the cave-man, reader of picture-writing,
be allowed to ponder over scientific truth. He
is at present the victim of the alleged truth of
the specious and sentimental variety of photograph. It gives the precise edges of the coat
or collar of the smirking masher and the exact
fibre in the dress of the jumping-jack. The
eye grows weary of sharp points and hard edges
that mean nothing. All this idiotic precision

is going to waste. It should be enlisted in the
cause of science and abated everywhere else.
The edges in art are as mysterious as in science
they are exact.

Some of the higher forms of the Intimate
Moving Picture play should be endowed by
local coteries representing their particular region. Every community of fifty thousand has
its group of the cultured who have heretofore
studied and imitated things done in the big
cities. Some of these coteries will in exceptional cases become creative and begin to express their habitation and name. The Intimate
Photoplay is capable of that delicacy and that
informality which should characterize neighborhood enterprises.

The plays could be acted by the group who,
season after season, have secured the opera
house for the annual amateur show. Other
dramatic ability could be found in the high-
schools. There is enough talent in any place
to make an artistic revolution, if once that
region is aflame with a common vision. The
spirit that made the Irish Players, all so racy
of the soil, can also move the company of local
photoplayers in Topeka, or Indianapolis, or
Denver. Then let them speak for their town,

not only in great occasional enterprises, but
steadily, in little fancies, genre pictures, de-
veloping a technique that will finally make
magnificence possible.

There was given not long ago, at the Illinois
Country Club here, a performance of The
Yellow Jacket by the Coburn Players. It at
once seemed an integral part of this chapter.

The two flags used for a chariot, the bamboo
poles for oars, the red sack for a decapitated
head, etc., were all convincing, through a direct
resemblance as well as the passionate acting.
They suggest a possible type of hieroglyphics to
be developed by the leader of the local group.

Let the enthusiast study this westernized
Chinese play for primitive representative
methods. It can be found in book form, a most
readable work. It is by G. C. Hazelton, Jr.,
and J. H. Benrimo. The resemblance between
the stage property and the thing represented
is fairly close. The moving flags on each side of
the actor suggest the actual color and progress
of the chariot, and abstractly suggest its magnificence. The red sack used for a bloody head
has at least the color and size of one. The
dressed-up block of wood used for a child is the
length of an infant of the age described and

wears the general costume thereof.   The farmer's hoe, though exaggerated, is still an agricultural implement.

The evening's list of properties is economical,
filling one wagon, rather than three.   Photographic realism is splendidly put to rout by
powerful representation.   When the villager
desires to embody some episode that if realistically given would require a setting beyond
the means of the available endowment, and
does not like the near-Egyptian method, let
him evolve his near-Chinese set of symbols.

The Yellow Jacket was written after long
familiarity with the Chinese Theatre in San
Francisco.   The play is a glory to that city as
well as to Hazleton and Benrimo.   But every
town in the United States has something as
striking as the Chinese Theatre, to the man
who keeps the eye of his soul open.   It has its
Ministerial Association, its boys' secret society,
its red-eyed political gang, its grubby Justice
of the Peace court, its free school for the teaching of Hebrew, its snobbish chapel, its fire-
engine house, its milliner's shop.   All these
could be made visible in photoplays as flies are
preserved in amber.

Edgar Lee Masters looked about him and

discovered the village graveyard, and made it as wonderful as Noah's Ark, or Adam naming the animals, by supplying honest inscriptions to the headstones. Such stories can be told by the Chinese theatrical system as well. As many different films could be included under the general title: "Seven Old Families, and Why they Went to Smash." Or a less ominous series would be "Seven Victorious Souls." For there are triumphs every day under the drab monotony of an apparently defeated town: conquests worthy of the waving of sun-banners.

Above all, The Yellow Jacket points a moral for this chapter because there was conscience behind it. First: the rectitude of the Chinese actors of San Francisco who kept the dramatic tradition alive, a tradition that was bequeathed from the ancient generations. Then the artistic integrity of the men who readapted the tradition for western consumption, and their religious attitude that kept the high teaching and devout feeling for human life intact in the play. Then the zeal of the Drama League that indorsed it for the country. Then the earnest work of the Coburn Players who embodied it devoutly, so that the whole company became dear friends forever.

By some such ladder of conscience as this
can the local scenario be endowed, written,
acted, filmed, and made a real part of the community life. The Yellow Jacket was a drama,
not a photoplay. This chapter does not urge
that it be readapted for a photoplay in San
Francisco or anywhere else. But a kindred
painting-in-motion, something as beautiful and
worthy and intimate, in strictly photoplay
terms, might well be the flower of the work of
the local groups of film actors.

Harriet Monroe's magazine, "Poetry" (Chicago), has given us a new sect, the Imagists:—
Ezra Pound, Richard Aldington, John Gould
Fletcher, Amy Lowell, F. S. Flint, D. H.
Lawrence, and others. They are gathering
followers and imitators. To these followers I
would say: the Imagist impulse need not be
confined to verse. Why would you be imitators of these leaders when you might be creators
in a new medium? There is a clear parallel-
ism between their point of view in verse and
the Intimate-and-friendly Photoplay, especially
when it is developed from the standpoint of the
last part of chapter nine, *space measured without sound plus time measured without sound.*

There is no clan to-day more purely devoted

to art for art's sake than the Imagist clan. An Imagist film would offer a noble challenge to the overstrained emotion, the overloaded splendor, the mere repetition of what are at present the finest photoplays. Now even the masterpieces are incontinent. Except for some of the old one-reel Biographs of Griffith's beginning, there is nothing of Doric restraint from the best to the worst. Read some of the poems of the people listed above, then imagine the same moods in the films. Imagist photoplays would be Japanese prints taking on life, animated Japanese paintings, Pompeian mosaics in kaleidoscopic but logical succession, Beardsley drawings made into actors and scenery, Greek vase-paintings in motion.

Scarcely a photoplay but hints at the Imagists in one scene. Then the illusion is lost in the next turn of the reel. Perhaps it would be a sound observance to confine this form of motion picture to a half reel or quarter reel, just as the Imagist poem is generally a half or quarter page. A series of them could fill a special evening.

The Imagists are colorists. Some people do not consider that photographic black, white, and gray are color. But here for instance are

seven colors which the Imagists might use:
(1) The whiteness of swans in the light.   (2) The
whiteness of swans in a gentle shadow.   (3) The
color of a sunburned man in the light.   (4) His
color in a gentle shadow.   (5) His color in a
deeper shadow.   (6) The blackness of black
velvet in the light.   (7) The blackness of black
velvet in a deep shadow.   And to use these
colors with definite steps from one to the other
does not militate against an artistic mystery
of edge and softness in the flow of line.   There
is a list of possible Imagist textures which is
only limited by the number of things to be
seen in the world.   Probably only seven or
ten would be used in one scheme and the same
list kept through one production.

The Imagist photoplay will put discipline
into the inner ranks of the enlightened and
remind the sculptors, painters, and architects
of the movies that there is a continence even
beyond sculpture and that seas of realism may
not have the power of a little well-considered
elimination.

The use of the scientific film by established
institutions like schools and state governments
has been discussed. Let the Church also, in
her own way, avail herself of the motion picture,

whole-heartedly, as in mediæval time she took over the marvel of Italian painting. There was a stage in her history when religious representation was by Byzantine mosaics, noble in color, having an architectural use, but curious indeed to behold from the standpoint of those who crave a sensitive emotional record. The first paintings of Cimabue and Giotto, giving these formulas a touch of life, were hailed with joy by all Italy. Now the Church Universal has an opportunity to establish her new painters if she will. She has taken over in the course of history, for her glory, miracle plays, Romanesque and Gothic architecture, stained glass windows, and the music of St. Cecilia's organ. Why not this new splendor? The Cathedral of St. John the Divine, on Morningside Heights, should establish in its crypt motion pictures as thoroughly considered as the lines of that building, if possible designed by the architects thereof, with the same sense of permanency.

This chapter does not advocate that the Church lay hold of the photoplays as one more medium for reillustrating the stories of the Bible as they are given in the Sunday-school papers. It is not pietistic simpering that will feed the spirit of Christendom, but a steady church-patronage of the most skilful and original motion picture artists.   Let the Church follow the precedent which finally gave us Fra Angelico, Botticelli, Andrea del Sarto, Leonardo da Vinci, Raphael, Michelangelo, Correggio, Titian, Paul Veronese, Tintoretto, and the rest.

Who will endow the successors of the present woman's suffrage film, and other great crusading films?   Who will see that the public documents and university researches take on the form of motion pictures?   Who will endow the local photoplay and the Imagist photoplay?   Who will take the first great measures to insure motion picture splendors in the church?

Things such as these come on the winds of to-morrow.   But let the crusader look about him, and where it is possible, put in the diplomatic word, and coöperate with the Gray Norns.

CHAPTER XVIII

ARCHITECTS AS CRUSADERS

MANY a worker sees his future America as a Utopia, in which his own profession, achieving dictatorship, alleviates the ills of men. The militarist grows dithyrambic in showing how war makes for the blessings of peace. The economic teacher argues that if we follow his political economy, none of us will have to economize. The church-fanatic says if all churches will merge with his organization, none of them will have to try to behave again. They will just naturally be good. The physician hopes to abolish the devil by sanitation. We have our Utopias. Despite levity, the present writer thinks that such hopes are among the most useful things the earth possesses.

A normal man in the full tide of his activities finds that a world-machinery could logically be built up by his profession. At least in the heyday of his working hours his vocation satisfies his heart. So he wants the entire human

race to taste that satisfaction. Approximate
Utopias have been built from the beginning.
Many civilizations have had some dominant
craft to carry them the major part of the way.
The priests have made India. The classical
student has preserved Old China to its present
hour of new life. The samurai knights have
made Japan. Sailors have evolved the British
Empire. One of the enticing future Americas
is that of the architect. Let the architect ap-
propriate the photoplay as his means of propaganda and begin. From its intrinsic genius
it can give his profession a start beyond all
others in dominating this land. Or such is one
of many speculations of the present writer.

The photoplay can speak the language of the
man who has a mind World's Fair size. That
we are going to have successive generations of
such builders may be reasonably implied from
past expositions. Beginning with Philadelphia
in 1876, and going on to San Francisco and San
Diego in 1915, nothing seems to stop us from
the habit. Let us enlarge this proclivity into
a national mission in as definite a movement,
as thoroughly thought out as the evolution of
the public school system, the formation of the
Steel Trust, and the like. After duly weighing

all the world's fairs, let our architects set about making the whole of the United States into a permanent one. Supposing the date to begin the erection be 1930. Till that time there should be tireless if indirect propaganda that will further the architectural state of mind, and later bring about the elucidation of the plans while they are being perfected. For many years this America, founded on the psychology of the Splendor Photoplay, will be evolving. It might be conceived as a going concern at a certain date within the lives of men now living, but it should never cease to develop.

To make films of a more beautiful United States is as practical and worth while a custom as to make military spy maps of every inch of a neighbor's territory, putting in each fence and cross-roads. Those who would satisfy the national pride with something besides battle flags must give our people an objective as shining and splendid as war when it is most glittering, something Napoleonic, and with no outward pretence of excessive virtue. We want a substitute as dramatic internationally, yet world-winning, friend making. If America is to become the financial centre through no fault of her own, that fact must have a symbol other than guns on the sea-coast.

If it is inexpedient for the architectural patriarchs and their young hopefuls to take over the films bodily, let a board of strategy be formed who make it their business to eat dinner with the scenario writers, producers, and owners, conspiring with them in some practical way.

Why should we not consider ourselves a deathless Panama-Pacific Exposition on a coast-to-coast scale? Let Chicago be the transportation building, Denver the mining building. Let Kansas City be the agricultural building and Jacksonville, Florida, the horticultural building, and so around the states.

Even as in mediæval times men rode for hundreds of miles through perils to the permanent fairs of the free cities, the world-travellers will attend this exhibit, and many of them will in the end become citizens. Our immigration will be something more than tide upon tide of raw labor. The Architects would send forth publicity films which are not only delineations of a future Cincinnati, Cleveland, or St. Louis, but whole counties and states and groups of states could be planned at one time, with the development of their natural fauna, flora, and forestry. Wherever nature has been rendered desolate by industry or mere haste, there let the architect and park-architect proclaim the plan. Wherever she is still splendid and untamed, let her not be violated.

America is in the state of mind where she must visualize herself again. If it is not possible to bring in the New Jerusalem to-day, by public act, with every citizen eating bread and honey under his vine and fig-tree, owning forty acres and a mule, singing hymns and saying prayers all his leisure hours, it is still reasonable to think out tremendous things the American people can do, in the light of what they have done, without sacrificing any of their native cussedness or kick. It was sprawling Chicago that in 1893 achieved the White City. The automobile routes bind the states together closer than muddy counties were held in 1893. A "Permanent World's Fair" may be a phrase distressing to the literal mind. Perhaps it would be better to say "An Architect's America."

Let each city take expert counsel from the architectural demigods how to tear out the dirty core of its principal business square and erect a combination of civic centre and per-

manent and glorious bazaar. Let the public
debate the types of state flower, tree, and
shrub that are expedient, the varieties of villages and middle-sized towns, farm-homes, and
connecting parkways.

Sometimes it seems to me the American
expositions are as characteristic things as our
land has achieved.   They went through without
hesitation.   The difficulties of one did not deter
the erection of the next.   The United States may
be in many things slack.   Often the democracy
looks hopelessly shoddy.   But it cannot be
denied that our people have always risen to the
dignity of these great architectural projects.

Once the population understand they are
dealing with the same type of idea on a grander
scale, they will follow to the end. We are not
proposing an economic revolution, or that
human nature be suddenly altered. If California
can remain in the World's Fair state of mind for
four or five years, and finally achieve such a splendid result, all the states can undertake a similar
project conjointly, and because of the momentum of a nation moving together, remain in that
mind for the length of the life of a man.

Here we have this great instrument, the
motion picture, the fourth largest industry in

the United States, attended daily by ten million people, and in ten days by a hundred million, capable of interpreting the largest conceivable ideas that come within the range of the plastic arts, and those ideas have not been supplied. It is still the plaything of newly rich vaudeville managers. The nation goes daily, through intrinsic interest in the device, and is dosed with such continued stories as the Adventures of Kathlyn, What Happened to Mary, and the Million Dollar Mystery, stretched on through reel after reel, week after week. Kathlyn had no especial adventures. Nothing in particular happened to Mary. The million dollar mystery was: why did the millionaires who owned such a magnificent instrument descend to such silliness and impose it on the people? Why cannot our weekly story be henceforth some great plan that is being worked out, whose history will delight us? For instance, every stage of the building of the Panama Canal was followed with the greatest interest in the films. But there was not enough of it to keep the films busy.

The great material projects are often easier to realize than the little moral reforms. Beautiful architectural undertakings, while appearing

to be material, and succeeding by the laws of
American enterprise, bring with them the healing hand of beauty.   Beauty is not directly
pious, but does more civilizing in its proper
hour than many sermons or laws.

The world seems to be in the hands of adventurers.   Why not this for the adventure of
the American architects?   If something akin
to this plan does not come to pass through
photoplay propaganda, it means there is no
American builder with the blood of Julius Cæsar
in his veins.   If there is the old brute lust for
empire left in any builder, let him awake.   The
world is before him.

As for the other Utopians, the economist,
the physician, the puritan, as soon as the architects have won over the photoplay people,
let these others take sage counsel and ensnare
the architects.   Is there a reform worth while
that cannot be embodied and enforced by a
builder's invention?   A mere city plan, carried
out, or the name or intent of a quasi-public
building and the list of offices within it may bring
about more salutary economic change than all
the debating and voting imaginable.   So without too much theorizing, why not erect our
new America and move into it?

CHAPTER XIX

ON COMING FORTH BY DAY

IF he will be so indulgent with his author, let the reader approach the photoplay theatre as though for the first time, having again a new point of view. Here the poorest can pay and enter from the glaring afternoon into the twilight of an Ali Baba's cave. The dime is the single open-sesame required. The half-light wherein the audience is seated, by which they can read in an emergency, is as bright and dark as that of some candle-lit churches. It reveals much in the faces and figures of the audience that cannot be seen by common day. Hard edges are the main things that we lose. The gain is in all the delicacies of modelling, tone-relations, form, and color. A hundred evanescent impressions come and go. There is often a tenderness of appeal about the most rugged face in the assembly. Humanity takes on its sacred aspect. It is a crude mind that would insist that these appearances are not real, that the eye does not see them when all eyes behold them. To say dogmatically that any new thing seen by half-light is an illusion, is like arguing that a discovery by the telescope or microscope is unreal. If the appearances are beautiful besides, they are not only facts, but assets in our lives.

Book-reading is not done in the direct noon-sunlight. We retire to the shaded porch. It takes two more steps toward quietness of light to read the human face and figure. Many great paintings and poems are records of things discovered in this quietness of light.

It is indeed ironical in our Ali Baba's cave to see sheer everydayness and hardness upon the screen, the audience dragged back to the street they have escaped. One of the inventions to bring the twilight of the gathering into brotherhood with the shadows on the screen is a simple thing known to the trade as the fade-away, that had its rise in a commonplace fashion as a method of keeping the story from ending with the white glare of the empty screen. As a result of the device the figures in the first episode emerge from the dimness and in the last one go back into the shadow whence they came, as foam returns to the darkness of an evening sea. In the imaginative pictures the principle begins to be applied more largely, till throughout the fairy story the figures float in and out from the unknown, as fancies should. This method in its simplicity counts more to keep the place an Ali Baba's cave than many a more complicated procedure. In luxurious scenes it brings the soft edges of Correggio, and in solemn ones a light and shadow akin to the effects of Rembrandt.

Now we have a darkness on which we can paint, an unspoiled twilight. We need not call it the Arabian's cave. There is a tomb we might have definitely in mind, an Egyptian burying-place where with a torch we might enter, read the inscriptions, and see the illustrations from the Book of the Dead on the wall, or finding that ancient papyrus in the mummy-case, unroll it and show it to the eager assembly, and have the feeling of return. Man is an Egyptian first, before he is any other type of civilized being. The Nile flows through his heart. So let this cave be Egypt, let us incline ourselves to revere the unconscious memories that echo within us when we see the hieroglyphics of Osiris, and Isis. Egypt was our long brooding youth. We built the mysteriousness

of the Universe into the Pyramids, carved it
into every line of the Sphinx. We thought always of the immemorial.

The reel now before us is the mighty judgment roll dealing with the question of our
departure in such a way that any man who
beholds it will bear the impress of the admoni-
tion upon his heart forever. Those Egyptian
priests did no little thing, when amid their
superstitions they still proclaimed the Judgment. Let no one consider himself ready for
death, till like the men by the Nile he can
call up every scene, face with courage every
exigency of the ordeal.

There is one copy of the Book of the Dead of
especial interest, made for the Scribe Ani, with
exquisite marginal drawings. Copies may be
found in our large libraries. The particular
fac-simile I had the honor to see was in the
Lenox Library, New York, several years ago.
Ani, according to the formula of the priesthood, goes through the adventures required of
a shade before he reaches the court of Osiris.
All the Egyptian pictures on tomb-wall and
temple are but enlarged picture-writing made
into tableaus. Through such tableaus Ani
moves. The Ani manuscript has so fascinated

some of the Egyptologists that it is copied in figures fifteen feet high on the walls of two of the rooms of the British Museum. And you can read the story eloquently told in Maspero.

Ani knocks at many doors in the underworld. Monstrous gatekeepers are squatting on their haunches with huge knives to slice him if he cannot remember their names or give the right password, or by spells the priests have taught him, convince the sentinels that he is Osiris himself. To further the illusion the name of Osiris is inscribed on his breast. While he is passing these perils his little wife is looking on by a sort of clairvoyant sympathy, though she is still alive. She is depicted mourning him and embracing his mummy on earth at the same time she accompanies him through the shadows.

Ani ploughs and sows and reaps in the fields of the underworld. He is carried past a dreadful place on the back of the cow Hathor. After as many adventures as Browning's Childe Roland he steps into the judgment-hall of the gods. They sit in majestic rows. He makes the proper sacrifices, and advances to the scales of justice. There he sees his own heart weighed against the ostrich-feather of Truth, by the jackal-god Anubis, who has already presided at his embalming. His own soul, in the form of a human-headed hawk, watches the ceremony. His ghost, which is another entity, looks through the door with his little wife. Both of them watch with tense anxiety. The fate of every phase of his personality depends upon the purity of his heart.

Lying in wait behind Anubis is a monster, part crocodile, part lion, part hippopotamus. This terror will eat the heart of Ani if it is found corrupt. At last he is declared justified. Thoth, the ibis-headed God of Writing, records the verdict on his tablet. The justified Ani moves on past the baffled devourer, with the mystic presence of his little wife rejoicing at his side. They go to the awful court of Osiris. She makes sacrifice with him there. The God of the Dead is indeed a strange deity, a seated semi-animated mummy, with all the appurtenances of royalty, and with the four sons of Horus on a lotus before him, and his two wives, Isis and Nephthys, standing behind his throne with their hands on his shoulders.

The justified soul now boards the boat in which the sun rides as it journeys through the night. He rises a glorious boatman in the morning, working an oar to speed the craft through the high ocean of the noon sky. Henceforth he makes the eternal round with the sun. Therefore in Ancient Egypt the roll was called, not the Book of the Dead, but *The Chapters on Coming Forth by Day.*

This book on motion pictures does not profess to be an expert treatise on Egyptology as well. The learned folk are welcome to amend the modernisms that have crept into it. But the fact remains that something like this story in one form or another held Egypt spell-bound for many hundred years. It was the force behind every mummification. It was the reason for the whole Egyptian system of life, death, and entombment, for the man not embalmed could not make the journey. So the explorer finds the Egyptian with a roll of this papyrus as a guide-book on his mummy breast. The soul needed to return for refreshment periodically to the stone chamber, and the mummy mutilated or destroyed could not entertain the guest. Egypt cried out through thousands of years for the ultimate resurrection of the whole man, his *coming forth by day.*

We need not fear that a story that so dominated a race will be lost on modern souls when

vividly set forth.   Is it too much to expect that
some American prophet-wizard of the future
will give us this film in the spirit of an Egyptian priest?

The Greeks, the wisest people in our limited
system of classics, bowed down before the
Egyptian hierarchy.   That cult must have
had a fine personal authority and glamour to
master such men.   The unseen mysteries were
always on the Egyptian heart as a burden and
a consolation, and though there may have
been jugglers in the outer courts of these
temples, as there have been in the courts of all
temples, no mere actor could make an Egyptian
priest of himself.   Their very alphabet has a
regal enchantment in its lines, and the same
æsthetic-mystical power remains in their py-
lons and images under the blaze of the all-
revealing noonday sun.

Here is a nation, America, going for dreams
into caves as shadowy as the tomb of Queen
Thi.   There they find too often, not that ancient
priestess and ruler, nor any of her kin, nor yet
Ani the scribe, nor yet any of the kings, but
shabby rags of fancy, or circuses that were
better in the street.

Because ten million people daily enter into

the cave, something akin to Egyptian wizardry, certain national rituals, will be born. By studying the matter of being an Egyptian priest for a little while, the author-producer may learn in the end how best to express and satisfy the spirit-hungers that are peculiarly American. It is sometimes out of the oldest dream that the youngest vision is born.

CHAPTER XX

THE whirlwind of cowboys and Indians with which the photoplay began, came about because this instrument, in asserting its genius, was feeling its way toward the most primitive forms of life it could find.

Now there is a tendency for even wilder things. We behold the half-draped figures living in tropical islands or our hairy fore-fathers acting out narratives of the stone age. The moving picture conventionality permits an abbreviation of drapery. If the primitive setting is convincing, the figure in the grass-robe or buffalo hide at once has its rights over the healthful imagination.

There is in this nation of moving-picture-goers a hunger for tales of fundamental life that are not yet told. The cave-man longs with an incurable homesickness for his ancient day. One of the fine photoplays of primeval life is the story called Man's Genesis, described in chapter two.

We face the exigency the world over of vast instruments like national armies being played against each other as idly and aimlessly as the checker-men on the cracker-barrels of corner groceries. And this invention, the kinetoscope, which affects or will affect as many people as the guns of Europe, is not yet understood in its powers, particularly those of bringing back the primitive in a big rich way. The primitive is always a new and higher beginning to the man who understands it. Not yet has the producer learned that the feeling of the crowd is patriarchal, splendid. He imagines the people want nothing but a silly lark.

All this apparatus and opportunity, and no immortal soul! Yet by faith and a study of the signs we proclaim that this lantern of wizard-drama is going to give us in time the visible things in the fulness of their primeval force, and some that have been for a long time invisible. To speak in a metaphor, we are going to have the primitive life of Genesis, then all that evolution after: Exodus, Leviticus, Numbers, Deuteronomy, Joshua, Judges, and on to a new revelation of St. John. In this adolescence of Democracy the history of man is to be retraced, the same round on a higher spiral of life.

Our democratic dream has been a middle-class aspiration built on a bog of toil-soddened minds. The piles beneath the castle of our near-democratic arts were rotting for lack of folk-imagination. The Man with the Hoe had no spark in his brain. But now a light is blazing. We can build the American soul broad-based from the foundations. We can begin with dreams the veriest stone-club warrior can understand, and as far as an appeal to the eye can do it, lead him in fancy through every phase of life to the apocalyptic splendors.

This progress, according to the metaphor of this chapter, will be led by prophet-wizards. These were the people that dominated the cave-men of old. But what, more specifically, are prophet-wizards?

Let us consider two kinds of present-day people: scientific inventors, on the one hand, and makers of art and poetry and the like, on the other. The especial producers of art and poetry that we are concerned with in this chapter we will call prophet-wizards: men like Albert Dürer, Rembrandt, Blake, Elihu Vedder,

Watts, Rossetti, Tennyson, Coleridge, Poe, Maeterlinck, Yeats, Francis Thompson.

They have a certain unearthly fascination in some one or many of their works. A few other men might be added to the list. Most great names are better described under other categories, though as much beloved in their own way. But these are especially adapted to being set in opposition to a list of mechanical inventors that might be called realists by contrast: the Wright brothers, and H. Pierpont Langley, Thomas A. Edison, Charles Steinmetz, John Hays Hammond, Hudson Maxim, Graham Bell.

The prophet-wizards are of various schools. But they have a common tendency and character in bringing forth a type of art peculiarly at war with the realistic civilization science has evolved. It is one object of this chapter to show that, when it comes to a clash between the two forces, the wizards should rule, and the realists should serve them.

The two functions go back through history, sometimes at war, other days in alliance. The poet and the scientist were brethren in the centuries of alchemy. Tennyson, bearing in mind such a period, took the title of Merlin in his veiled autobiography, Merlin and the Gleam.

Wizards and astronomers were one when the angels sang in Bethlehem, "Peace on Earth, Good Will to Men." There came magicians, saying, "Where is he that is born king of the Jews, for we have seen his star in the east and have come to worship him?" The modern world in its gentler moments seems to take a peculiar thrill of delight from these travellers, perhaps realizing what has been lost from parting with such gentle seers and secular diviners. Every Christmas half the magazines set them forth in richest colors, riding across the desert, following the star to the same manger where the shepherds are depicted.

Those wizard kings, whatever useless charms and talismans they wore, stood for the unknown quantity in spiritual life. A magician is a man who lays hold on the unseen for the mere joy of it, who steals, if necessary, the holy bread and the sacred fire. He is often of the remnant of an ostracized and disestablished priesthood. He is a free-lance in the soul-world, owing final allegiance to no established sect. The fires of prophecy are as apt to descend upon him as upon members of the established faith.

He loves the mysterious for the beauty of it, the wildness and the glory of it, and not always to compel stiff-necked people to do right.

It seems to me that the scientific and poetic functions of society should make common cause again, if they are not, as in Merlin's time, combined in one personality. They must recognize that they serve the same society, but with the understanding that the prophetic function is the most important, the wizard vocation the next, and the inventors' and realists' genius important indeed, but the third consideration. The war between the scientists and the prophet-wizards has come about because of the half-defined ambition of the scientists to rule or ruin. They give us the steam-engine, the skyscraper, the steam-heat, the flying machine, the elevated railroad, the apartment house, the newspaper, the breakfast food, the weapons of the army, the weapons of the navy, and think that they have beautified our existence.

Moreover some one rises at this point to make a plea for the scientific imagination. He says the inventor-scientists have brought us the mystery of electricity, which is no hocus-pocus, but a special manifestation of the Imma-

nent God within us and about us. He says
the student in the laboratory brought us the
X-ray, the wireless telegraph, the mystery of
radium, the mystery of all the formerly unharnessed power of God which man is beginning
to gather into the hollow of his hand.

The one who pleads for the scientific imagination points out that Edison has been called
the American Wizard. All honor to Edison and
his kind. And I admit specifically that Edison
took the first great mechanical step to give us
the practical kinetoscope and make it possible
that the photographs, even of inanimate objects
thrown upon the mirror-screen, may become
celestial actors. But the final phase of the
transfiguration is not the work of this inventor
or any other. As long as the photoplays are in
the hands of men like Edison they are mere
voodooism. We have nothing but Moving
Day, as heretofore described. It is only in
the hands of the prophetic photoplaywright
and allied artists that the kinetoscope reels
become as mysterious and dazzling to the thinking spirit as the wheels of Ezekiel in the first
chapter of his prophecy. One can climb into
the operator's box and watch the sword-like
stream of light till he is as dazzled in flesh

and spirit as the moth that burns its wings in the lamp. But this is while a glittering vision and not a mere invention is being thrown upon the screen.

The scientific man can explain away the vision as a matter of the technique of double exposure, double printing, trick-turning, or stopping down. And having reduced it to terms and shown the process, he expects us to become secular and casual again. But of course the sun itself is a mere trick of heat and light, a dynamo, an incandescent globe, to the man in the laboratory. To us it must be a fire upon the altar.

Transubstantiation must begin. Our young magicians must derive strange new pulse-beats from the veins of the earth, from the sap of the trees, from the lightning of the sky, as well as the alchemical acids, metals, and flames. Then they will kindle the beginning mysteries for our cause. They will build up a priesthood that is free, yet authorized to freedom. It will be established and disestablished according to the intrinsic authority of the light revealed.

Now for a closer view of this vocation.

The picture of Religious Splendor has its

obvious form in the delineation of Biblical
scenes, which, in the hands of the best commercial producers, can be made as worth while
as the work of men like Tissot. Such films are
by no means to be thought of lightly. This sort
of work will remain in the minds of many of
the severely orthodox as the only kind of a
religious picture worthy of classification. But
there are many further fields.

Just as the wireless receiving station or the
telephone switchboard become heroes in the
photoplay, so Aaron's rod that confounded the
Egyptians, the brazen serpent that Moses up-
lifted in the wilderness, the ram's horn that
caused the fall of Jericho, the mantle of Elijah
descending upon the shoulders of Elisha from
the chariot of fire, can take on a physical elec-
trical power and a hundred times spiritual
meaning that they could not have in the dead
stage properties of the old miracle play or the
realism of the Tissot school. The waterfall and
the tossing sea are dramatis personæ in the
ordinary film romance. So the Red Sea overwhelming Pharaoh, the fires of Nebuchadnezzar's
furnace sparing and sheltering the three holy
children, can become celestial actors. And
winged couriers can appear, in the pictures,

with missions of import, just as an angel descended to Joshua, saying, "As captain of the host of the Lord am I now come."

The pure mechanic does not accept the doctrine. "Your alleged supernatural appearance," he says, "is based on such a simple fact as this: two pictures can be taken on one film."

But the analogy holds. Many primitive peoples are endowed with memories that are double photographs. The world faiths, based upon centuries of these appearances, are none the less to be revered because machine-ridden men have temporarily lost the power of seeing their thoughts as pictures in the air, and for the time abandoned the task of adding to tradition.

Man will not only see visions again, but machines themselves, in the hands of prophets, will see visions. In the hands of commercial men they are seeing alleged visions, and the term *"vision"* is a part of moving-picture studio slang, unutterably cheapening religion and tradition. When Confucius came, he said one of his tasks was the rectification of names. The leaders of this age should see that this word *"vision"* comes to mean something more than a piece

of studio slang. If it is the conviction of
serious minds that the mass of men shall never
again see pictures out of Heaven except through
such mediums as the kinetoscope lens, let all
the higher forces of our land courageously lay
hold upon this thing that saves us from perpetual spiritual blindness.

When the thought of primitive man, embodied
in misty forms on the landscape, reached epic
proportions in the Greek, he saw the Olympians
more plainly than he beheld the Acropolis.
Myron, Polykleitos, Phidias, Scopas, Lysippus,
Praxiteles, discerned the gods and demigods
so clearly they afterward cut them from the
hard marble without wavering. Our guardian
angels of to-day must be as clearly seen and
nobly hewn.

A double mental vision is as fundamental
in human nature as the double necessity for
air and light. It is as obvious as that a thing
can be both written and spoken. We have
maintained that the kinetoscope in the hands
of artists is a higher form of picture writing.
In the hands of prophet-wizards it will be a
higher form of vision-seeing.

I have said that the commercial men are
seeing alleged visions. Take, for instance, the

large Italian film that attempts to popularize
Dante. Though it has a scattering of noble
passages, and in some brief episodes it is an
enhancement of Gustave Doré, taking it as a
whole, it is a false thing. It is full of apparitions worked out with mechanical skill, yet
Dante's soul is not back of the fires and swords
of light. It gives to the uninitiated an outline of the stage paraphernalia of the Inferno.
It has an encyclopædic value. If Dante
himself had been the high director in the pleni-
tude of his resources, it might still have had
that hollowness. A list of words making a
poem and a set of apparently equivalent pictures
forming a photoplay may have an entirely
different outcome. It may be like trying to
see a perfume or listen to a taste. Religion
that comes in wholly through the eye has a
new world in the films, whose relation to the
old is only discovered by experiment and intui-
tion, patience and devotion.

But let us imagine the grandson of an Italian
immigrant to America, a young seer, trained
in the photoplay technique by the high American masters, knowing all the moving picture
resources as Dante knew Italian song and
mediæval learning. Assume that he has a

genius akin to that of the Florentine. Let him
be a Modernist Catholic if you will. Let him
begin his message in the timber lands of Minne-
sota or the forests of Alaska. "In midway of
this our mortal life I found me in a gloomy
wood astray." Then let him paint new pictures of just punishment beyond the grave, and
merciful rehabilitation and great reward. Let
his Hell, Purgatory, and Paradise be built of
those things which are deepest and highest in
the modern mind, yet capable of emerging in
picture-writing form.

Men are needed, therefore they will come.
And lest they come weeping, accursed, and
alone, let us ask, how shall we recognize them?
There is no standard by which to discern the
true from the false prophet, except the mood
that is engendered by contemplating the mes-
sengers of the past. Every man has his own
roll call of noble magicians selected from the
larger group. But here are the names with
which this chapter began, with some words on
their work.

Albert Dürer is classed as a Renaissance
painter. Yet his art has its dwelling-place in
the early Romanesque savageness and strangeness. And the reader remembers Dürer's

brooding muse called Melancholia that so
obsessed Kipling in The Light that Failed.
But the wonder-quality went into nearly all
the Dürer wood-cuts and etchings. Rembrandt is a prophet-wizard, not only in his
shadowy portraits, but in his etchings of holy
scenes even his simplest cobweb lines become
incantations. Other artists in the high tides
of history have had kindred qualities, but
coming close to our day, Elihu Vedder, the
American, the illustrator of the Rubáiyát, found
it a poem questioning all things, and his very
illustrations answer in a certain fashion with
winds of infinity, and bring the songs of Omar
near to the Book of Job. Vedder's portraits
of Lazarus and Samson are conceptions that
touch the hem of the unknown. George Frederick Watts was a painter of portraits of the
soul itself, as in his delineations of Burne-Jones
and Morris and Tennyson.

It is a curious thing that two prophet-wizards
have combined pictures and song. Blake and
Rossetti, whatever the failure of their technique,
never lacked in enchantment. Students of
the motion picture side of poetry would
naturally turn to such men for spiritual precedents. Blake, that strange Londoner, in his

book of Job, is the paramount example of the enchanter doing his work with the engraving tool in his hand.

Rossetti's Dante's Dream is a painting on the edge of every poet's paradise. As for the poetry of these two men, there are Blake's Songs of Innocence, and Rossetti's Blessed Damozel and his Burden of Nineveh.

As for the other poets, we have Coleridge, the author of Christabel, that piece of winter witchcraft, Kubla Khan, that oriental dazzlement, and the Ancient Mariner, that most English of all this list of enchantments. Of Tennyson's work, besides Merlin and the Gleam, there are the poems when the mantle was surely on his shoulders: The Lady of Shalott, The Lotus Eaters, Sir Galahad, and St. Agnes' Eve.

Edgar Poe, always a magician, blends this power with the prophetical note in the poem, The Haunted Palace, and in the stories of William Wilson, The Black Cat and The Tell-tale Heart. This prophet-wizard side of a man otherwise a wizard only, has been well illustrated in The Avenging Conscience photoplay.

From Maeterlinck we have The Bluebird and many another dream. I devoutly hope

I will never see in the films an attempt to paraphrase this master. But some disciple of his should conquer the photoplay medium, giving us great original works.

Yeats has bestowed upon us The Land of Heart's Desire, The Secret Rose, and many another piece of imaginative glory. Let us hope that we may be spared any attempts to hastily paraphrase his wonders for the motion pictures. But the man that reads Yeats will be better prepared to do his own work in the films, or to greet the young new masters when they come.

Finally, Francis Thompson, in The Hound of Heaven, has written a song that the young wizard may lean upon forevermore for private guidance. It is composed of equal parts of wonder and conscience. With this poem in his heart, the roar of the elevated railroad will be no more in his ears, and he will dream of palaces of righteousness, and lead other men to dream of them till the houses of mammon fade away.

CHAPTER XXI

THE ACCEPTABLE YEAR OF THE LORD

WITHOUT airing my private theology I earnestly request the most sceptical reader of this book to assume that miracles in a Biblical sense have occurred. Let him take it for granted in the fashion of the strictly æsthetic commentator who writes in sympathy with a Fra Angelico painting, or as that great modernist, Paul Sabatier, does as he approaches the problems of faith in the life of St. Francis. Let him also assume, for the length of time that he is reading this chapter if no longer, that miracles, in a Biblical sense, as vivid and as real to the body of the Church, will again occur two thousand years in the future : events as wonderful as those others, twenty centuries back. Let us anticipate that many of these will be upon American soil. Particularly as sons and daughters of a new country it is a spiritual necessity for us to look forward to traditions, because we have so few from the

306 THE ART OF THE MOVING PICTURE

past identified with the six feet of black earth beneath us.

The functions of the prophet whereby he definitely painted future sublimities have been too soon abolished in the minds of the wise. Mere forecasting is left to the weather bureau so far as a great section of the purely literary and cultured are concerned. The term prophet has survived in literature to be applied to men like Carlyle: fiery spiritual leaders who speak with little pretence of revealing to-morrow.

But in the street, definite forecasting of future events is still the vulgar use of the term. Dozens of sober historians predicted the present war with a clean-cut story that was carried out with much faithfulness of detail, considering the thousand interests involved. They have been called prophets in a congratulatory secular tone by the man in the street. These felicitations come because well-authorized merchants in futures have been put out of countenance from the days of Jonah and Balaam till now. It is indeed a risky vocation. Yet there is an undeniable line of successful forecasting by the hardy, to be found in the Scripture and in history. In direct proportion as these men of fiery speech were free from sheer silliness, their outlook has been considered and debated by the gravest people round them.   The heart of man craves the seer.   Take, for instance, the promise of the restoration of Jerusalem in glory that fills the latter part of the Old Testament. It moves the Jewish Zionist, the true race-Jew, to this hour.   He is even now endeavoring to fulfil the prophecy.

Consider the words of John the Baptist, "One mightier than I cometh, the latchet of whose shoes I am not worthy to unloose: he shall baptize you with the Holy Ghost and with fire."   A magnificent foreshadowing, being both a spiritual insight and the statement of a great definite event.

The heeded seers of the civilization of this our day have been secular in their outlook. Perhaps the most striking was Karl Marx, in the middle of the capitalistic system tracing its development from feudalism and pointing out as inevitable, long before they came, such modern institutions as the Steel Trust and the Standard Oil Company.   It remains to be seen whether the Marxian prophecy of the international alliance of workingmen that is obscured by the present conflict in Europe, and other of his forecastings, will be ultimately verified.

There have been secular teachers like Darwin, who, by a scientific reconstruction of the past, have implied an evolutionary future based on the biological outlook. Deductions from the teachings of Darwin are said to control those who mould the international doings of Germany and Japan.

There have been inventor-seers like Jules Verne. In Twenty Thousand Leagues under the Sea he dimly discerned the submarine. There is a type of social prophet allied to Verne. Edward Bellamy, in Looking Backward, reduced the world to a matter of pressing the button, turning on the phonograph. It was a combination of glorified department-store and Coney Island, on a coöperative basis. A seventeen-year-old boy from the country, making his first visit to the Woolworth building in New York, and riding in the subway when it is not too crowded, might be persuaded by an eloquent city relative that this is Bellamy's New Jerusalem.

A soul with a greater insight is H. G. Wells. But he too, in spite of his humanitarian heart, has, in a great mass of his work, the laboratory imagination. Serious Americans pronounce themselves beneficiaries of Wells' works,

and I confess myself edified and thoroughly
grateful. Nevertheless, one smells chemicals
in the next room when he reads most of Wells'
prophecies. The X-ray has moved that Englishman's mind more dangerously than moon-
light touches the brain of the chanting witch.
One striking and typical story is The Food
of the Gods. It is not only a fine speculation,
but a great parable. The reader may prefer
other tales. Many times Wells has gone into
his laboratory to invent our future, in the same
state of mind in which an automobile manu-
facturer works out an improvement in his car.
His disposition has greatly mellowed of late, in
this respect, but underneath he is the same
Wells.

Citizens of America, wise or foolish, when
they look into the coming days, have the submarine mood of Verne, the press-the-button
complacency of Bellamy, the wireless telegraph enthusiasm of Wells. If they express
hopes that can be put into pictures with definite
edges, they order machinery piled to the skies.
They see the redeemed United States running
deftly in its jewelled sockets, ticking like a
watch.

This, their own chosen outlook, wearies the

imaginations of our people, they do not know why. It gives no full-orbed apocalyptic joy. Only to the young mechanical engineer does such a hope express real Utopia. He can always keep ahead of the devices that herald its approach. No matter what day we attain and how busy we are adjusting ourselves, he can be moving on, inventing more to-morrows; ruling the age, not being ruled by it.

Because this Utopia is in the air, a goodly portion of the precocious boys turn to mechanical engineering. Youths with this bent are the most healthful and inspiring young citizens we have. They and their like will fulfil a multitude of the hopes of men like Verne, Bellamy, and Wells.

But if every mechanical inventor on earth voiced his dearest wish and lived to see it worked out, the real drama of prophecy and fulfilment, as written in the imagination of the human race, would remain uncompleted.

As Mrs. Browning says in Lady Geraldine's Courtship: —

If we trod the deeps of ocean, if we struck the stars in
    rising,
If we wrapped the globe intensely with one hot electric
    breath,

'Twere but power within our tether, no new spirit-power
    comprising,
And in life we were not greater men, nor bolder men in
    death.

St. John beheld the New Jerusalem coming down out of Heaven prepared as a bride adorned for her husband, not equipped as a touring car varnished for its owner.

It is my hope that the moving picture prophet-wizards will set before the world a new group of pictures of the future. The chapter on The Architect as a Crusader endeavors to show how, by proclaiming that America will become a permanent World's Fair, she can be made so within the lives of men now living, if courageous architects have the campaign in hand. There are other hopes that look a long way further. They peer as far into the coming day as the Chinese historian looks into the past. And then they are but halfway to the millennium.

Any standard illustrator could give us Verne or Bellamy or Wells if he did his best. *But we want pictures beyond the skill of any delineator in the old mediums, yet within the power of the wizard photoplay producer.* Oh you who are coming to-morrow, show us every-

day America as it will be when we are only
halfway to the millennium yet thousands of
years in the future! Tell what type of honors
men will covet, what property they will still
be apt to steal, what murders they will com-
mit, what the law court and the jail will be or
what will be the substitutes, how the newspaper
will appear, the office, the busy street.

Picture to America the lovers in her half-
millennium, when usage shall have become
iron-handed once again, when noble sweet-
hearts must break beautiful customs for the
sake of their dreams. Show us the gantlet
of strange courtliness they must pass through
before they reach one another, obstacles brought
about by the immemorial distinctions of scholar-
ship gowns or service badges.

Make a picture of a world where machinery
is so highly developed it utterly disappeared
long ago. Show us the antique United States,
with ivy vines upon the popular socialist
churches, and weather-beaten images of socialist saints in the niches of the doors. Show
us the battered fountains, the brooding universities, the dusty libraries. Show us houses
of administration with statues of heroes in
front of them and gentle banners flowing from

their pinnacles. Then paint pictures of the oldest trees of the time, and tree-revering ceremonies, with unique costumes and a special priesthood.

Show us the marriage procession, the christening, the consecration of the boy and girl to the state. Show us the political processions and election riots. Show us the people with their graceful games, their religious pantomimes. Show us impartially the memorial scenes to celebrate the great men and women, and the funerals of the poor. And then moving on toward the millennium itself, show America after her victories have been won, and she has grown old, as old as the Sphinx. Then give us the Dragon and Armageddon and the Lake of Fire.

Author-producer-photographer, who would prophesy, read the last book in the Bible, not to copy it in form and color, but that its power and grace and terror may enter into you. Delineate in your own way, as you are led on your own Patmos, the picture of our land redeemed. After fasting and prayer, let the Spirit conduct you till you see in definite line and form the throngs of the brotherhood of man, the colonnades where the arts are expounded, the gardens where the children dance.

That which man desires, that will man
become. He largely fulfils his own prediction
and vision. Let him therefore have a care how
he prophesies and prays. We shall have a tin
heaven and a tin earth, if the scientists are
allowed exclusive command of our highest
hours.

Let us turn to Luke iv. 17.

"And there was delivered unto him the book
of the prophet Esaias. And when he had opened
the book he found the place where it was
written : —

" The Spirit of the Lord is upon me because
he hath anointed me to preach the Gospel to the
poor; he hath sent me to heal the broken-
hearted, to preach deliverance to the captives,
and recovering of sight to the blind, to set at
liberty them that are bruised, to preach the
acceptable year of the Lord.

"And he closed the book, and he gave it
again to the minister, and sat down. And the
eyes of all them that were in the synagogue
were fastened on him. And he began to say
unto them: 'This day is this Scripture fulfilled in your ears.'

"And all bare him witness, and wondered
at the gracious words which proceeded out

of his mouth. And they said: 'Is not this Joseph's son?'"

I am moved to think Christ fulfilled that prophecy because he had read it from childhood. It is my entirely personal speculation, not brought forth dogmatically, that Scripture is not so much inspired as it is curiously and miraculously inspiring.

If the New Isaiahs of this time will write their forecastings in photoplay hieroglyphics, the children in times to come, having seen those films from infancy, or their later paraphrases in more perfect form, can rise and say, "This day is this Scripture fulfilled in your ears." But without prophecy there is no fulfilment, without Isaiah there is no Christ.

America is often shallow in her dreams because she has no past in the European and Asiatic sense. Our soil has no Roman coin or buried altar or Buddhist tope. For this reason multitudes of American artists have moved to Europe, and only the most universal of wars has driven them home. Year after year Europe drained us of our beauty-lovers, our highest painters and sculptors and the like. They have come pouring home, confused expatriates, trying to adjust themselves. It is time for the American craftsman and artist to grasp the fact that we must be men enough to construct a to-morrow that grows rich in forecastings in the same way that the past of Europe grows rich in sweet or terrible legends as men go back into it.

*　*　*　*　*　*

Scenario writers, producers, photoplay actors, endowers of exquisite films, sects using special motion pictures for a predetermined end, all you who are taking the work as a sacred trust, I bid you God-speed. Let us resolve that whatever America's to-morrow may be, she shall have a day that is beautiful and not crass, spiritual, not material. Let us resolve that she shall dream dreams deeper than the sea and higher than the clouds of heaven, that she shall come forth crowned and transfigured with her statesmen and wizards and saints and sages about her, with magic behind her and miracle before her.

Pray that you be delivered from the temptation to cynicism and the timidities of orthodoxy. Pray that the workers in this your glorious new art be delivered from the mere lust of the flesh and pride of life. Let your spirits outflame your burning bodies.

Consider what it will do to your souls, if you are true to your trust. Every year, despite earthly sorrow and the punishment of your mortal sins, despite all weakness and all of Time's revenges upon you, despite Nature's reproofs and the whips of the angels, new visions will come, new prophecies will come. You will be seasoned spirits in the eyes of the wise. The record of your ripeness will be found in your craftsmanship. You will be God's thoroughbreds.

*   *   *   *   *   *

It has come then, this new weapon of men, and the face of the whole earth changes. In after centuries its beginning will be indeed remembered.

It has come, this new weapon of men, and by faith and a study of the signs we proclaim that it will go on and on in immemorial wonder.

VACHEL LINDSAY.

Springfield, Illinois,
    Nov. 1, 1915.

Printed in the United States of America.

INDEX